Fun with
Miniature Log Cabin Blocks
featuring 20 charming quilts

Donna Fite McConnell

Dedication

To Micah, my daughter and friend, who encourages me when I need it and always gives me confidence. When I asked her to sign a friendship block for me, she wrote, "To my Mother, you are my hero." I feel the same about her.

Acknowledgments

To those at That Patchwork Place, especially Ursula Reikes, Nancy Martin, who had faith in me, and Marion Shelton, who has been a good friend and a great giver of encouragement, which was so much a part of my getting this book written. They patiently waited for more than two years for me to get my health and priorities in order, so I could finally get down to the business of writing this book. They didn't give up on me during my struggle with the beginning stages of fibromyalgia, which contributed to my lack of focus. Starting this book was the hardest part. Now that it is finished, I thank you.

And finally, my heartfelt thanks to Christine Barnes, who through her outstanding editorial skills, was able to cut, compress, and mold my words into the work you see here.

A Special Thank-You

To my husband, Father Gary. When I was writing *Lively Little Logs* five years ago, I dedicated my book to him because of his encouragement and support, even though he had to deal with unprepared meals and unsewn buttons. Last night, I walked into the kitchen, and there he sat, with his little sewing box, sewing buttons onto a pair of pants. Although the conditions around here have not changed, he continues to praise my work, rally me on, and run my errands.

Gary, I love you.

Credits

Technical Editor	✿	Christine Barnes
Design & Production Manager	✿	Cheryl Stevenson
Cover Designer	✿	Magrit Baurecht
Text Designer	✿	Kay Green
Copy Editor	✿	Liz McGehee
Illustrator	✿	Lisa McKenney
Photographer	✿	Brent Kane

Fun with Miniature Log Cabin Blocks
© 1998 by Donna Fite McConnell

Martingale & Company,
PO Box 118,
Bothell, WA 98041-0118 USA

Printed in Canada
03 02 01 00 99 98   6 5 4 3 2 1

Library of Congress Cataloging-in-Publication Data
McConnell, Donna Fite,
    Fun with miniature log cabin blocks : featuring 20 charming quilts / Donna Fite McConnell.
        p. cm.
    ISBN 1-56477-230-6
    1. Patchwork—Patterns. 2. Machine appliqué—Patterns. 3. Machine quilting. I. Title.
TT835.M2755 1998
746.46'041—dc21   98-18128
                                                            CIP

MISSION STATEMENT

We are dedicated to providing quality products and service by working together to inspire creativity and to enrich the lives we touch.

Contents

Preface

I have been surrounded by quilts all of my life. My grandmother was an avid quiltmaker, and we always had warm quilts on our beds. But it was not until 1981 that quilts made a difference in my life.

I signed up for a quilting class, thinking that I would make a quilt for my home, and discovered that there was much more to quiltmaking than just stitching a few quilts. The joy of achievement, the pleasure of performance, and the satisfaction of creating something new are gratifying feelings that come from finishing a quilt.

One of the joys I have discovered in my life as a quiltmaker is the power of friendship and the feelings of connection that quiltmaking provides. I have seen this as I have trekked around the country to quilt shows and to workshops I taught from my first book, Lively Little Logs. I have made numerous friends and enjoy seeing them again and again in my travels.

My closest supporters are not only members of my family, who always cheer me on, but also members of my quilt groups here in Arkansas. These friendships have enriched my life in many ways and taught me a lot about achievement, fulfillment, success, and tradition.

I will never be able to repay the many people who have brought joy to my life, but I hope that those of you who appreciate my work will get some reward from using my patterns. I offer them to you as a "thank-you" and trust that you will enjoy making them as much as I delighted in the process of creating them.

I worked with techniques in these projects that were new to me. I found that I love working on foundations. I enjoyed experimenting with different-size logs in the same block, and I loved working with the photo-transfer process. I discovered that stretching our creativity is what keeps us inspired, and learning new techniques and approaches enhances our performance.

My quilts reflect my personality, and I encourage you, as you make my designs, to add something to each quilt that mirrors who you are. Use your favorite colors. Combine attributes of different quilts to make your quilts truly your own.

I offer this book to each of you, my family and friends, who have enriched, inspired, and gladdened my heart.

Enjoy,
Donna Fite McConnell

Introduction

I hope that you will use *Fun with Miniature Log Cabin Blocks* as a workbook. Read the entire book, especially the basic directions, before beginning the projects. Many of the quilts use different techniques from the ones I used in the past, and those guidelines will be included in the directions for each quilt.

At the end of nearly every project, you'll find a space for "Notes." Use this space as you would a journal and record anything you need to remember, such as setting changes you made on your machine. List different threads or fabrics you used. Make a note of the date you made the project, who it was for, how many hours you spent making it, and any pertinent information you might want to keep. Be sure to take a photo of your finished quilt and keep it in your book. With all of this information, you'll have a reference if you wish to make a project again.

Throughout the book I have included tips to make your sewing a little easier and a lot more fun. It is my intention to help you develop better ways of doing the techniques I have used. I am open to suggestions and willing to learn new ways to improve my work. The process of quiltmaking is what most of us enjoy, and my wish is that you enjoy making these quilts as much as I did.

Meet the Author

Donna Fite McConnell is a quilt designer, teacher, and author. She has self-published a number of her designs as patterns and is the author of *Lively Little Logs*, her first book for That Patchwork Place.

Donna started her career as a shop owner, teaching tole and decorative painting. She now spends her time designing and making quilts, teaching, and lecturing. Her background in decorative painting has influenced her use of color and detail in her work.

Donna's quilts have been published in numerous national magazines and books. Her patterns have been featured in *Better Homes and Gardens' American Patchwork and Quilting* (August 1995) and Leisure Arts, Inc., publications. Articles have appeared in *Miniature Quilts* (Summer 1991), *Quilting Today*, (April 1993), and *Mini Quilts* by Anita Murphy and Her Friends.

Her quilts and accessories may also be found in Anita Hallock's *Fast Patch*, Harriet Hargrave's *Mastering Machine Appliqué*, and Rodale Press's *America's Best Quilting Projects*.

Donna and friend Pat Eaton were honored with the purchase of their quilt, "Our Secret Garden," by the Museum of the American Quilter's Society in Paducah, Kentucky. "Our Secret Garden" has appeared on the cover of *The American Quilter* (Summer 1991), in the Journal of AIQA (Fall 1991), in *Quilt* magazine (Summer 1993), on the cover of the *Catalog of Books of the American Quilter's Society* (1992), and in the Lang Graphics's 1992 *Calendar of American Quilts of AIQA*.

Donna is the wife of the Rev. Dr. Gary McConnell, rector of Trinity Parish Church in Searcy, Arkansas. She and Father Gary have three grown children and one very special granddaughter.

Organization

Quiltmaking is relaxing, rewarding, and just plain fun. Sometimes, however, we get frustrated because we start a project without planning ahead. If you take a little time before you begin a project to organize your work, you will save time in the long run. We can also become so excited about a project that we jump right in without reading all of the directions. This eagerness wastes fabric and time. Following are tips to help make your next project a pleasure and a success.

- Before you begin, clean up your sewing area and put away all materials and supplies used in previous projects.
- Collect everything you need on the materials list.
- Start with a new needle. For foundation piecing, a 90/14 needle perforates the paper well and makes removal easy. If you are using the strip-piecing method, use an 80/12 needle.
- As you follow the directions, check off each step as you finish it.

Equipment and Supplies

I was told, years ago, that my work can be only as good as the quality of my equipment. Whether you are quilting, sewing, cooking, or painting, always buy the best tools you can afford. I use the following equipment and supplies at home and at workshops.

Sewing Machine and Accessories

A good-quality sewing machine is probably the most important tool for machine appliqué and machine quilting. You don't need to rush out and buy a new, top-of-the-line machine if yours is in good working order. However, a machine that has ongoing tension problems or jams the thread will interfere with the joy of quiltmaking and will not give you pleasing results. Following are important features:

- Machine appliqué requires a zigzag stitch. Some machines also have a stitch setting that resembles a hand-stitched blanket stitch. You can usually adjust the width and length of this stitch from its preset position to produce a stitch that looks like delicate hand stitching.

- The ability to lower the feed dogs is an important feature for free-motion quilting.
- Having the needle stop in the down position helps to hold the layers together when you raise the presser foot. This feature enables you to turn your work as you machine appliqué and quilt.
- Easy tension adjustment and the ability to use different-weight thread in the bobbin and through the needle simultaneously are helpful features.
- A machine that does not overheat after long periods of sewing makes it possible to keep working.

Knowing how to use your machine is important. If classes are offered where you purchased your machine, take advantage of them. Check the manual if you don't know how to perform a function.

Clean and oil your machine frequently. If you use your machine for long periods, as I do, brush out the lint and oil the machine after approximately fifteen hours of sewing. Some people like to remove the lint each time the bobbin runs out. Whichever method you prefer, stick to it. Regular cleaning will keep your machine running for years.

DARNING FOOT. This foot is necessary for free-motion quilting such as stippling and quilting around machine appliqué.

OPEN-TOE EMBROIDERY FOOT. This foot is essential for machine appliqué because it allows you to see where you are stitching. Use it to machine quilt straight lines on small quilts.

EVEN-FEED OR WALKING FOOT. On larger quilts, it is easier to hold the layers together if you use an even-feed or walking foot.

QUILTER'S ¼" FOOT. This little foot is a tremendous help for machine piecing, but you still must check your work for accurate seam allowances.

Tip: To check your ¼" seam allowance, take three strips, each 1½" wide, and sew them together; press. The center strip should measure 1"; if not, make adjustments until it does. Note any modifications so you can continue to sew accurate seams.

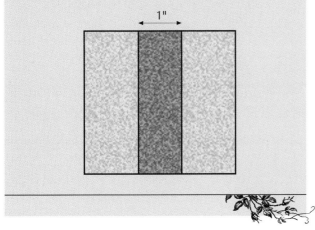

IRON AND IRONING PAD. My choice is a lightweight travel iron that I can easily pack for workshops. When I sew, I like to have my iron set up to the right of my machine so I can press each seam without getting up. I prefer the pressing pad that has a cushioned pad on one side and a cutting mat on the other.

Rotary Equipment and Scissors

The larger-size rotary cutter works best. If you are not familiar with using a rotary cutter, be sure to follow the manufacturer's safety precautions. Keep extra blades on hand.

When cutting strips for Log Cabin blocks, I use a 3" x 18" clear-acrylic ruler. When squaring up the blocks, I use a Bias Square®. You will also need a rotary-cutting mat at your cutting table and a small mat beside your sewing machine.

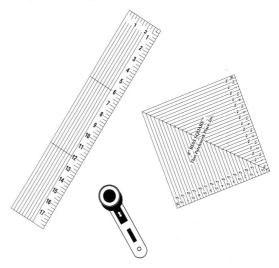

Scissors, 6" or 7", are great for some cutting, but since most of my cutting is done at the sewing machine, I use 4" embroidery scissors. In fact, I keep them in my hand while I am sewing. They are useful for clipping threads and for trimming pieces before and after they are sewn to a foundation.

Use utility scissors for cutting paper in foundation piecing and for cutting fusible web and freezer paper.

General Supplies

LIGHT. I keep a small lamp near my machine. Good light makes for less stress. Also, when working with paper foundation piecing, it's helpful to hold your paper up to the light to align seam allowances.

QUILTING PINS. Use the glass-head pins; they are thinner and easier to use.

TRACING PAPER. Use tracing paper, available at art-supply stores, to draw or trace foundations.

NOTEBOOK. If you do not use the "Notes" section at the end of most projects, keep a notebook and record your machine settings, where you purchased the fabrics, needle sizes, date you completed your project, and so on.

PENS AND PENCILS. Use permanent pens for adding details to quilts, making labels, and signing your work. A heat-transfer pen is useful for drawing foundation blocks, especially if you are making multiples of the same block.

Fabric-marking pencils come in colors that show on both dark and light fabrics; most wash out. Washaway and air-evaporating pens are useful for marking quilting lines. I like to use the purple pen to mark lines for machine quilting. Be aware, however, that the lines disappear in about twenty-four hours, so don't mark any more than you can quilt in a day.

REMOVABLE OR MASKING TAPE. Use removable tape or masking tape to hold the tracing paper to the pattern and to hold fabric pieces to the foundation. Tape is a good quilting guide for hand quilting, but remove it immediately after you have quilted along its edge to avoid leaving residue on the quilt.

BAGS. Store your appliqué pieces and other small pieces in plastic bags that seal.

PAPER-BACKED FUSIBLE WEB. I recommend the lightest-weight web; it is sold on the bolt or in packages of precut pieces.

TEAR-AWAY STABILIZER. Use this stabilizer behind the background fabric when doing machine appliqué. Tear-Easy, Stitch-n-Tear, or HeatnBond are some of the available brands.

LIGHT BOX. A light box is helpful for appliqué and for tracing quilting designs and quilt labels. It is also useful for lining up the strips in foundation piecing.

SAFETY PINS. Use size 00 brass safety pins or QuiltTak to baste the quilt sandwich.

TWEEZERS. Tweezers are handy for removing bits of paper from paper foundations and clipped threads from ripped-out seams.

Batting

Fairfield Cotton Classic, Pellon Fleece, Hobbs Heirloom Cotton, and Hobbs Thermore are the battings I use most. Needlepunch cotton battings are my favorite.

A lightweight, low-loft batting without buoyancy is best for machine quilting. Cotton batting is a good choice because it lies flat. Follow the manufacturer's directions for prewashing cotton batting.

Fabric

Use only 100%-cotton fabrics. Fabrics with any polyester tend to shrink when pressed, a feature that can ruin your quilt if the strips are narrower than 1".

Choosing fabrics is an ongoing process, and most devoted quilters have an ever-growing collection. Because fabric manufacturers bring out new lines several times a year, we see new fabrics that we "just have to have." If that's the case, buy it. I am frequently asked about a fabric in one of my quilts and where to get it. Unfortunately, most fabrics are discontinued after short lives, and when it's gone, it's gone.

Don't be afraid to experiment with color and use what you like. Remember, when choosing fabrics for Log Cabin blocks, the value—the lightness or darkness of a color—is what establishes the design. You will need definite darks and definite lights. Avoid placing medium-value colors side by side; they tend to blend when viewed from a distance.

If you want a pastel look, try using two soft colors, one for each side of the Log Cabin block. Pink and blue—or peach and green—are pleasing combinations. With this approach, you can use lighter values and still define the two sides of the block.

Border-Stripe Fabrics

On small quilts, borders with tiny stripes can make the difference between an ordinary quilt and a stunning one. Border-stripe fabrics, with the stripes running lengthwise, are ideal for the borders on my quilts.

Yardage

You can make most of the designs in this book from fabrics left over from other projects. It is unlikely that you will need more than ½ yard of any one fabric for a project, with the exception of "Sunshine and Shadows" (page 88). I recommend buying ⅛-yard pieces, if your shop will cut them. If not, buy ¼-yard pieces. Fat quarters are ideal for small projects like these.

I do not prewash my fabrics. I don't expect my little quilts to need washing, and I like the way new fabric feels. If I were making a quilt that would get lots of wear, I would prewash my fabrics.

Thread

Always use the best quality thread you can afford. Although it is all right to use up leftover thread from other projects, do not use the inexpensive, short-fiber thread sold at discount stores. It jams your machine, shrinks, and deteriorates over time.

- Neutral threads—tan, light gray, dark gray, etc.— work well for most piecing projects. Size 50 is a good weight for most cotton fabrics. The higher the number, the lighter the weight. For appliqué, machine-embroidery thread is best. One of my favorite threads for appliqué is DMC Broder Machine (machine embroidery), 50-weight, variegated thread. It comes in many colors. The two I use most are color #115 (a red-to-black shading that works well on red flowers) and color #111 (a yellow-to-gold that works well for flower centers).
- Monofilament thread (size .004) is fine enough for machine quilting. Use clear for light-background fabrics, and smoke for darker fabrics.
- Metallic thread is effective for quilting and embellishing.
- 60- or 70-weight polyester or cotton thread is a good choice in the bobbin when you use monofilament thread for quilting. Use colors to match your backing fabrics.

Resources

You can order 6" and 8" bell-pull hardware, full foundations (ready to sew) for each project in this book, photo transfer paper, and fabric directly from me. Contact me for a price list.

Donna's Designs
Donna Fite McConnell
105 North Apple Street
Searcy, AR 72143-5225
Phone: 501-268-1211
E-mail:donna@ipa.net

Making Log Cabin Blocks

Most Log Cabin quilts are made from blocks that are half light and half dark, with the lights and darks divided diagonally. In the traditional Log Cabin block, the light and dark logs are the same width. Many of the projects in this book use the traditional Log Cabin block. However, some have variations in log width and light-and-dark placement.

Traditional light/dark block

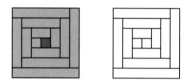

Light/dark variations in the traditional block

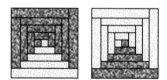

Light/dark variations in
bell-pull blocks (pages 34–36)

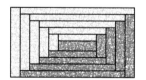

Rectangular block in
"Red Diamond with Stars" (page 42)

Uneven logs in
"Nobody Gets in to See
the Wizard . . ." (page 46)

Uneven logs in
"Angel" (page 37) and
"Cherry Blossom" (page 38)

Even though the light and dark sides may vary, Log Cabin blocks are constructed in the same manner: you add the "logs," or rows, in numerical order around the center square, traditionally called the "chimney." You can make Log Cabin blocks using either the foundation-piecing or strip-piecing method.

Foundation Piecing

"Everything old is new again." Remember that saying? Well, that's certainly true with foundation piecing. I remember my grandmother piecing on paper when I was a little girl; she called these quilts "string quilts." I thought foundation piecing was too slow when I first tried it, but the more I do, the more I enjoy it.

Carol Doak has written a number of books on foundation piecing, including *Show Me How to Paper Piece* (That Patchwork Place, 1997). She provides excellent instructions for many kinds of foundation-pieced blocks.

Piecing on a foundation will give you a perfect block every time as long as you sew on the lines and piece in numerical order. The foundation can be tracing paper, newsprint, copy paper, freezer paper, or tear-away stabilizer.

The foundations on pages 91–96 are full size and ready to use. You can reproduce the blocks by tracing them onto the foundation material of your choice or using a copy machine. It is all right to copy these foundations for your own use.

If you use a photocopy machine, measure the block on the copy to be sure no distortion has occurred. Usually, a copy from the original will be accurate enough, but if you try copying from copies, you will probably notice distortion.

Cut the strips across the width of the fabric from selvage to selvage. Cut the strips slightly wider than you would for other piecing methods to allow a little extra in the seam allowances. Add about ⅛" to your finished log size, plus two ¼"-wide seam allowances. For projects in this book, you will cut ⅞"-wide strips for ¼"-wide logs, and 1"-wide strips for ⅜"-wide logs. After you are accustomed to using this method, you may not need to add the extra width. Cut each strip long enough to include a little more than the seam allowances at each end.

 **Tip:** *Make a sample block before cutting all of the strips to see if the block looks the way you want it to look. If the seam allowances look skimpy, increase the strip width slightly.*

Foundation-Piecing Tips

🔖 When trimming seam allowances, keep the paper side toward you. Fold the paper down, on the line, before trimming the seam allowances to avoid cutting the foundation.

🔖 Set the stitch length at 18 or 20 stitches per inch.

🔖 Backstitching is not necessary; each seam crosses over the previous seam, securing the threads.

🔖 Use a neutral-color thread for both the light and dark fabrics.

🔖 When making several blocks of the same color combination, make one block as a sample, then piece the remaining blocks.

🔖 It is not necessary to use the same fabric for the same-numbered pieces in the blocks (the same blue print for all #4 logs, for example). I prefer to vary the fabrics from block to block for a scrappier look.

Pressing Techniques

The following pressing method prevents distortion of the little logs. Be sure to press each seam after sewing. Do not use steam.

1. Place the unopened unit on the ironing board, with the strip sewn last on top and the seam allowances away from you.
2. To set the stitches, put the iron straight down on the unit without moving the iron back and forth.
3. Lift the last-sewn strip to open the unit. Set the iron on the area of the block nearest you, then gently glide the iron toward the opened fabric, away from you.

Step-by-Step Foundation Piecing

Check each strip before sewing it to the foundation to make sure you are sewing a light strip to the light area, or a dark strip to the dark area.

1. Place the "chimney" square (Log #1) right side up so that it covers Square #1 on the unmarked (back) side of the paper. Allow a ¼" seam allowance on all sides beyond the sewing lines. Hold the foundation up to the light, checking from the marked side to make sure the piece is centered on Square #1.

 NOTE: You always place the chimney right side up, but all of the following pieces are placed right side down before sewing. Remember, the fabric is sewn to the unmarked (back) side of the paper foundation.

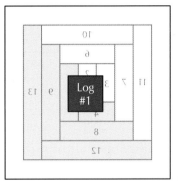

Unmarked (back) side;
Log #1 right side

2. Working on the unmarked side of the foundation, place the second square (Log #2) on top of the chimney square, right sides together. Use a pin or a piece of tape to hold the pieces in place if necessary.

3. Turn the paper foundation over, with the marked side up, and sew on the line that divides Square #1 and #2. Sew 1 or 2 stitches beyond the beginning and end of the line. Do not backstitch.

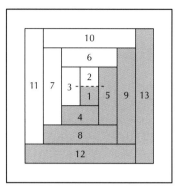

Marked side

4. Holding the paper foundation with the marked side facing up and the seam you just stitched toward the top of the block (north), fold the paper toward you on the sewn line. Trim the excess fabric, leaving a ¼" seam allowance.

5. Open Log #2 and finger-press by running your thumbnail across the seam. Press.

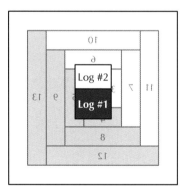

Logs #1 and #2 stitched and pressed

 NOTE: When you hold the block up to the light on the marked side, you should have ¼" seam allowances extending on all unsewn sides.

6. Working on the unmarked side, lay Log #3 across Logs #1 and #2, right sides together.

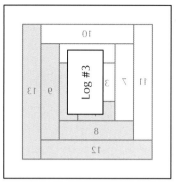

Unmarked side

7. Turn the foundation over and sew Log #3 (the second seam) on the marked line, stitching through all layers.

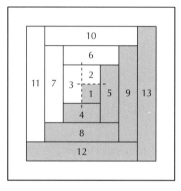

Marked side

Open Log #3 and press.

8. For the remaining logs, repeat the above steps, adding the pieces in numerical order until you complete the block.

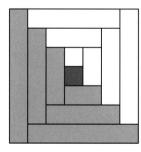

Completed block

9. Press the completed block from the right side.

10. Trim the excess fabric, leaving a ¼" seam allowance around the block.

Removing the Paper

Leave the paper on the blocks until you assemble the quilt; then remove it before quilting. Use a pair of sharp-pointed embroidery scissors or a stiletto to get under the paper. Gently pull away the paper. For the outside edges, fold the paper on the seam lines, creasing it with your thumbnail, and gently tear it away. If you have problems, spritz the paper with water or moisten slightly with a damp cloth.

Strip Piecing

With this Log Cabin method, you add the logs around the chimney in numerical order, just as you would for foundation piecing. But because there is no foundation, you can chain piece the blocks, sewing the same-numbered logs to the blocks consecutively without cutting the thread.

Rotary Cutting the Strips

1. If cutting your strips from yardage (not scraps or fat quarters), fold the fabric in half from the center fold to the selvages, creating 4 layers. Position the fabric on the cutting mat as shown.

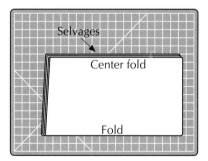

Selvages

Center fold

Fold

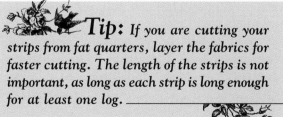

Tip: *If you are cutting your strips from fat quarters, layer the fabrics for faster cutting. The length of the strips is not important, as long as each strip is long enough for at least one log.*

2. To square up the cut edges of the fabric, place your square ruler on the fold and line up the long edge of your long ruler with the left edge of the square. Slide both items left or right until the right edge of the long ruler just covers the raw edges of the fabric.

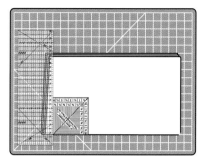

3. Remove the square ruler. Holding the long ruler firmly in place with your left hand, roll the rotary cutter across the fabric, along the ruler's edge. As a safety precaution, always roll the cutter away from you. Discard this strip.

4. Determine the width of the strip you are cutting and align the corresponding mark on the long ruler with the cut edge of the fabric. Cut the strip to the desired width.

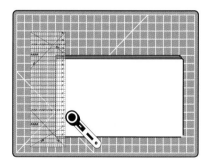

NOTE: The width of the strips in each strip-pieced project includes a ¼" seam allowance.

5. After every 2 or 3 cuts, check to see if the cut edge is still on the straight grain of the fabric. Fabric has a tendency to shift very slightly while cutting, and you may need to "true up" the edge after a few cuts. Using the square ruler and long ruler, make a cut to straighten the edge before cutting any more strips.

Piecing the Blocks

Use a stitch length of 12 to 14 stitches per inch. Accuracy is important when piecing with this method, so check your ¼" seam allowance (page 7) before you begin.

Add the rows, or "logs," in numerical order as shown in the illustration below.

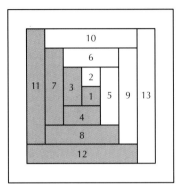

On most blocks, the center of the block, or "chimney," and the first log are the same size. Before sewing the first two strips together, determine the length of the strips by multiplying the number of blocks by the cut width of the strips. If, for example, you are using ¾"-wide strips and are making ten blocks, you will need ten ¾" "chimney" and first-log units, requiring strips at least 7½" long. I like to add an inch or two to the strip to allow for errors. It never hurts to make a few extra blocks just in case you make a mistake somewhere in the process.

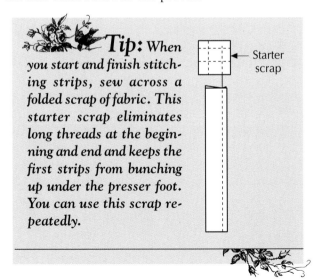

Tip: When you start and finish stitching strips, sew across a folded scrap of fabric. This starter scrap eliminates long threads at the beginning and end and keeps the first strips from bunching up under the presser foot. You can use this scrap repeatedly.

When making more than one block, use the following chain-piecing method.

1. With right sides together and raw edges even, sew the strips together along one edge, using a ¼"-wide seam allowance. Press the seam toward Log #2.

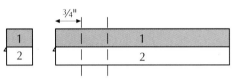

2. Using a rotary cutter and ruler, cut the sewn strips into units. Cut as many units as there are blocks in the quilt. For "Log Diamond with Floral Border" (page 26) and "Patriotic Heart" (page 70), cut the units ¾" wide. For "Sunshine and Shadows" (page 88), cut the units 1" wide.

Tip: *After cutting the units, stack them so all face in the same direction. Turn the stack over and place it beside the machine, with the blocks facing in the direction they will be fed into the machine. Make a habit of arranging your units this way after adding each log; it will help you avoid sewing the logs to the wrong side.*

3. Choose a strip for Log #3. (Be sure to check your block illustration to determine if you need a light or dark strip.) Lay this strip on the machine, right side up. Place the small units (Logs #1 and #2) right side down on the strip (Log #3), as close as possible without overlapping them. Sew the units to Log #3 along the right edge, using a ¼"-wide seam allowance. Log #2 should be closest to you as you feed the units through the machine.

4. Press the seam toward Log #3, the last strip sewn; then cut the blocks apart, using a rotary cutter and ruler.

5. Place the next strip, Log #4, right side up on the machine. Place the blocks, right side down, on top of the strip, as close together as possible without overlapping them. Log #3, the newest log, should be closest to you as you feed the blocks through the machine. Sew the blocks to Log #4.

6. Press the seams toward Log #4, the last strip sewn; then cut the blocks apart, using your rotary cutter and cutting guide.

7. Continue adding logs around the block in numerical order, following the illustration for color placement, until you have the number of rows needed. As you add each row, check your block measurement, being sure to include the seam allowances. If necessary, use a small 4" x 4" ruler or a Bias Square to trim the edges ever so slightly and square up the block.

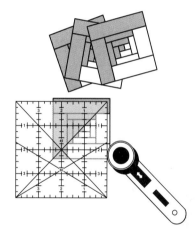

Machine Appliqué

I choose to machine appliqué because it is much less time-consuming than hand appliqué. Machine appliqué, when care is taken and it is well done, can be just as beautiful as hand appliqué. The method that follows uses fusible web to adhere the appliqué pieces to the background fabric.

Fusing

1. Lay the fusible web directly over the appliqué design and trace each piece onto the paper side of the web. Keep in mind that you are making a mirror image when you trace; you may need to reverse some pieces.

Tip: *When using words or letters, I find it easier to make plastic templates of the letters. I turn the letters over and trace them backwards onto the paper side of the web; then they will face correctly when I cut the fabric pieces.*

2. Using paper scissors, cut out the shapes from the fusible web, cutting slightly beyond the lines. (This is not a seam allowance.)

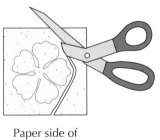

Paper side of
fusible web

3. Check the manufacturer's directions for the proper iron settings for fusing. Place the drawn shape on the wrong side of the fabric, web side down, and press.

4. After fusing all pieces to the wrong sides of your fabrics, cut out the shapes on the tracing lines. (Seam allowances are not necessary in machine appliqué.)

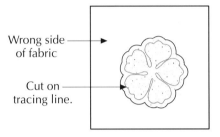

Wrong side
of fabric

Cut on
tracing line.

5. Remove the paper backing by scoring the paper at the center of the shape with a pin and peeling off the paper. It's easier to remove the paper if you let the pieces "rest" for at least 30 minutes after fusing.

6. Place the background on your ironing board and arrange the appliqué pieces on the background as shown in the quilt plan. (For some projects, the appliqué pieces are numbered in order of placement.) Fuse the pieces to the background with a hot iron, following the manufacturer's instructions carefully.

Tip: *Sometimes, when the appliqué pieces are very small, it's hard to see which side of the fabric has the fusible web. Take care that all pieces are right side up. A piece stuck to the bottom of the iron is very hard to remove.*

Setting Up Your Machine

Set your machine for a tiny satin zigzag or blanket stitch. Adjust the length and width of the stitch until you achieve the desired stitch. Set your machine for the needle to stop in the "down" position. Practice on a fabric scrap to find the setting you like.

Check the tension before beginning. To avoid seeing bobbin thread on top of your work, the tension should be slightly looser on the top thread or slightly tighter on the bobbin thread. Some machines have a small eye on the bobbin case that you can put the thread through to tighten the bobbin tension slightly.

Thread through extra eye.

You can use the same thread in the bobbin throughout the appliqué process if the thread doesn't show. If you can't keep the bobbin thread from showing, use the same color thread in the bobbin as you use on the top.

Appliquéing the Design

If you are new to machine appliqué, take a little time to practice before starting your project.

1. Place a piece of tear-away stabilizer, large enough to cover the area to be appliquéd, behind the background fabric. Use straight pins or hold it in place with your fingers until you start stitching.

2. Attach your open-toe embroidery foot. Choose threads to match the colors of the appliqué pieces for the top thread, and a neutral thread in the bobbin. Plan to appliqué the same-color pieces first.

3. Decide where you want to start stitching and lower the needle into the background, next to the fused piece. On a typical flower, appliqué the stem first, followed by the leaf and flower. Finish with the flower center.

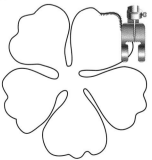

Using a satin stitch or blanket stitch, stitch over the raw edges of the piece so that the outside edge of the stitching penetrates the background fabric, and the inside edge goes into the design about $1/16$".

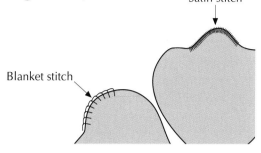

Satin stitch

Blanket stitch

Appliqué the pieces that will be underneath other pieces first. Do not stitch areas that will be hidden by overlapping pieces.

Work slowly as you stitch up to and around points. If you can adjust the width of your zigzag stitch, decrease the stitch width just before and after the point. Increase the stitch width to normal as you continue. Points take practice.

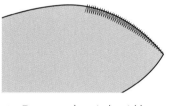

Decrease the stitch width as you work toward the point.

When stitching around a curve, let the needle hold the fabric in place as you lift the presser foot to turn the piece slightly. On outside curves, stop the needle on the outside of the curve to turn your work. On inside curves, stop the needle on the inside of the curve. This technique avoids gaps and gives solid stitch coverage.

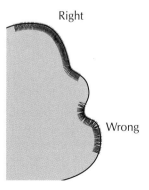

Right

Wrong

Continue appliquéing until you have stitched all pieces, changing thread colors as needed.

4. Remove the tear-away stabilizer; press.

Borders

I almost always put a narrow border, often black, next to the Log Cabin blocks and around the appliquéd borders. These narrow borders outline the blocks and frame the design. If the quilt does not have an appliquéd border, the second border is usually cut from a contrasting fabric or a border-stripe fabric (page 9).

All of the projects in this book use straight-cut borders.

1. Measure the length of the quilt top at the center from raw edge to raw edge. Cut 2 border strips to that measurement and mark the midpoints on the strips and the sides of the quilt top.

   Sew the border strips to the sides of the quilt, matching ends and midpoints and easing as necessary. Press seam allowances toward the border.

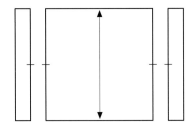

Mark midpoints.

2. Measure the width of the quilt top at the center from raw edge to raw edge, including the border strips just sewn to the sides. Cut 2 border strips to this measurement and mark the midpoints of the strips and the top and bottom edges of the quilt top. Sew the border strips to the quilt, matching ends and midpoints and easing as necessary. Press seam allowances toward the border.

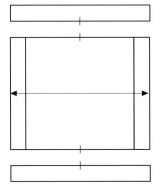

Mark midpoints.

Machine Quilting

Machine quilting, like hand quilting, becomes more beautiful with practice. Just as in hand quilting—where the goal is to quilt so many stitches to the inch, with even stitches on front and back—in machine quilting we strive to achieve even, straight rows of stitching. Free-motion quilting should be smooth, with even curves. Maurine Noble's *Machine Quilting Made Easy!* (That Patchwork Place, 1994) is a helpful guide.

Preparing the Quilt Sandwich

1. Cut the batting and backing fabric at least 2" larger than the quilt top on all sides. Press the backing fabric if necessary.
2. Lay the backing, wrong side up, on a table or work surface. Place the batting on top of the backing. Place the quilt top, right side up, on top of the batting to make the quilt "sandwich."
3. Smooth out any wrinkles and pin-baste the layers together, if necessary, using safety pins placed 4" to 5" apart.

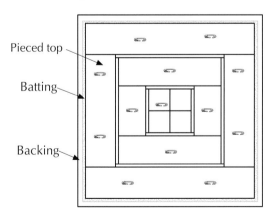

Pieced top

Batting

Backing

Quilting

Straight-line quilting is best for quilting in-the-ditch and continuous, straight lines. Raise the feed dogs and set your machine for a straight stitch and a stitch length of approximately 12 stitches per inch, or the preset length on your machine.

Thread your machine with monofilament thread on the top (size .004) and cotton or cotton-wrapped polyester thread, 60 to 70 weight, in the bobbin. Match the bobbin thread to the backing fabric.

Start in the center of the quilt and work out to the edges. When quilting in-the-ditch, quilt on the seam line, just on the side without the seam allowance. This technique helps bury the quilting in the seam.

Free-motion quilting allows you to guide the stitching by hand. Use a darning foot and lower the feed dogs or cover them so that you are in control of the needle. To prevent the threads from tangling underneath, bring the bobbin thread to the top before beginning.

Needle

Bobbin thread

Secure the ends of the thread by making a few stitches in one place. Then quilt a few stitches and snip the beginning threads.

Begin stitching, pushing the quilt in the desired direction but not turning it. Stitch at a medium speed and keep the quilt as flat as possible. Outline your design first; then go back and do fill-in stitching.

Echo quilting (successive rows of stitching around an appliqué piece to "echo" its shape) and stipple quilting (meandering lines of stitching) are both forms of free-motion quilting.

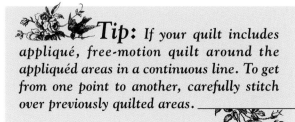

Tip: *If your quilt includes appliqué, free-motion quilt around the appliquéd areas in a continuous line. To get from one point to another, carefully stitch over previously quilted areas.*

Color Photo Transfers

You can use color copy machines for many kinds of transferring, including photos and printed messages. Color-copy transfers are permanent and washable, making it possible to create memory quilts for any occasion. Many copy centers will copy your photos onto transfer paper and even transfer the images to fabric. Some copy centers will do both; however, the cost is much higher. Following are directions for doing the steps yourself.

Copying the Images

You must use photo transfer paper, available at many quilt and hobby shops and copy centers. Follow the manufacturer's directions carefully. Use good-quality color photos or clean, clear printing for best results. You can copy several photos on one transfer sheet. Cut away any parts of the photo you do not want to transfer and tape the photos to a sheet of plain white copy paper with a small piece of double-sided tape. Place the photos as close together as possible, leaving ⅓" at the edges of the paper.

To transfer a message, print it on a sheet of paper and treat it like a photo.

Before you copy your photos or messages onto photo transfer paper, set the machine to reverse the image. Make a test copy on plain paper. Once you are satisfied with the result, manually feed the transfer paper, one sheet at a time, into the copier with the coated side of the paper facing correctly.

Transferring to Fabric

Use only 100%-cotton fabric with a tight weave.
1. Do not wash the fabric. Press to remove wrinkles. Avoid using the center fold of the fabric if you can't iron it completely flat. Remove any loose threads, lint, or fibers.
2. Cut the images apart, trimming anything you don't want to transfer.
3. Transfer one image at a time. Place the transfer, image side down, onto the fabric, lining up the image with the weave of the fabric. Leave at least 1" between each transfer.

4. Set your iron on the cotton setting without steam and lower your ironing board for better leverage. Press for 30 to 40 seconds. Bear down as hard as you can without sliding the iron back and forth. Lift the iron and move it slightly to avoid keeping the steam vents in the same spot.
5. Wait only a few seconds for the fabric to cool slightly. Peel away the paper from side to side, not from corner to corner. If the paper does not come off easily, repeat the pressing process.

 NOTE: When pressing transfers larger than the sole plate of your iron, press in sections, each for 30 or 40 seconds, as described above. Reheat the entire transfer, then peel off the paper all at once.

If you encounter problems with this transfer process, check the following:
- White spots on the photo may mean that you did not keep the iron on long enough, or you were using a rough fabric.
- If the paper did not release all of the image, you may not have applied enough pressure or allowed enough pressing time. Repeat the process.
- If the paper doesn't come off easily, you may have waited too long before trying to peel it off. Press for another 10 to 15 seconds and try again.
- If a paper jam occurs, be sure the photo transfer paper is not curled or bent. To avoid static electricity, remove the paper from its plastic bag several hours before using it and fan the paper.

Tip: *Wash photo transfers by hand in warm water. Press on the back of the fabric.*

A Word of Warning

Most professional photographs and pictures in books and magazines are copyrighted. To avoid embarrassment or legal problems, be sure to get permission before making copies of these images.

Finishing

Making a Sleeve

The bell pulls and wall quilts in this book all require a sleeve to insert a rod or hardware for hanging. If you choose to use bell-pull hardware, the quilt will need a sleeve at the top and the bottom.

The best way to add a sleeve is to attach it when you sew the binding.

1. Cut a strip of backing fabric 6" wide and 1" shorter than the finished width of the quilt. For bell pulls, cut 2 strips, each 4" wide and 1" shorter than the finished width of the bell pull.

2. Fold the short ends ¼" to the wrong side and press. Fold the edge ¼" again and stitch.

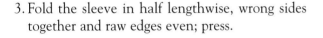

3. Fold the sleeve in half lengthwise, wrong sides together and raw edges even; press.

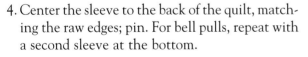

4. Center the sleeve to the back of the quilt, matching the raw edges; pin. For bell pulls, repeat with a second sleeve at the bottom.

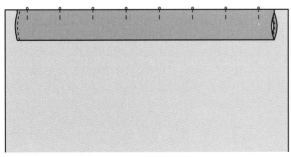

5. Sew the sleeve in place when you add the binding. Blindstitch the bottom fold of the sleeve to the backing.

Binding the Edges

Binding is the traditional finish for a quilt. Double-fold binding, cut on the crosswise grain, provides a crisp, stable edge.

1. Using your rotary cutter, carefully trim the edges of the quilt through all layers. Be sure the quilt is square; errors are more noticeable on a small quilt than a large one.

2. Measure the distance around the quilt to determine how much binding you need. Add 4" to 5" to this measurement for joining the strips, mitering the corners, and overlapping the ends.

3. Cut the binding strips 2" wide across the width of the fabric.

4. To make a long, continuous binding strip, join the ends of the strips at a 45° angle. Trim the excess fabric and press the seams open.

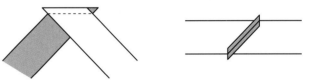

5. Fold the strip in half lengthwise, wrong sides together, and press. Unfold one end of the binding and turn under ¼" at a 45° angle to create a finished edge at the end of the binding.

Fold line

6. Use a walking foot to stitch the binding to the quilt. Starting in the middle of the bottom edge of the quilt, lay the binding strip on the front, with the raw edges even. Begin stitching approximately 1½" from the beginning of the binding, using a ¼"-wide seam allowance. Stop stitching ¼" from the edge of the quilt and backstitch.

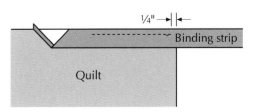

¼"

Binding strip

Quilt

7. Turn the quilt. Fold the binding up and away from the quilt at a 45° angle.

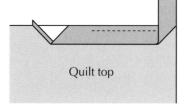

Quilt top

8. Fold the binding again, bringing it down along the edge of the quilt. The straight fold should be even with the top edge of the quilt. Put the needle into the quilt again ¼" from the top edge and continue stitching to the next corner.

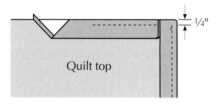

Quilt top

¼"

9. Repeat at each corner until you are approximately 2" to 3" from where you began stitching. Cut the binding, leaving a 1" overlap. Slip the just-cut end of the binding into the folded end and finish stitching.

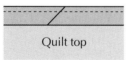

Quilt top

10. Fold the binding to the back of the quilt; the folded edge should just cover the machine stitching. Fold each corner to create a miter; pin if necessary. Blindstitch the binding by hand, making sure the stitches do not go through to the front.

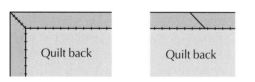

Quilt back   Quilt back

Adding Prairie Points

Prairie points are stitched to the front of the quilt. If you plan to use prairie points, do not trim the batting and backing as you would for binding. Leave approximately 2" of the outer border unquilted at the edge so you can fold it back to stitch the prairie points.

1. Cut the squares, each 1½" x 1½". Fold the squares in half diagonally, then in half diagonally again; press.

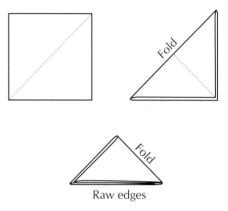

Fold

Fold

Raw edges

2. On the back of the quilt, fold the batting and backing out of the way and secure with quilting pins.

Quilt top   Batting   Backing

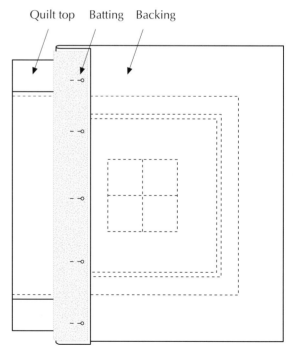

3. Working on the right side of the quilt top, place a folded triangle ½" from the corner on one side, with the raw edges even. Stitch the prairie point, using a ¼"-wide seam allowance, about halfway. Stop with the needle in the down position.

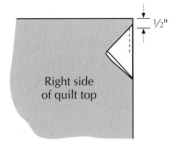

4. Slip another prairie point about ¼" into the fold of the first prairie point; continue stitching about halfway on the second prairie point.

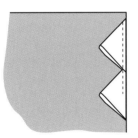

5. Continue adding and stitching prairie points, choosing colors at random, until you reach the corner. You may need to adjust the last few points for fit. Place the last prairie point about ½" from the corner of the quilt so you can press the points out without having to fold any portion of the last triangle. Continue until all prairie points are added.

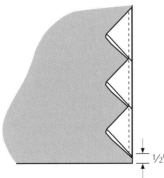

6. From the right side, press the prairie points away from the center. The seam allowance will naturally turn to the wrong side of the quilt top.

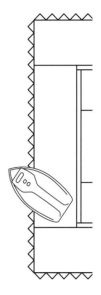

7. Turn the quilt over and smooth the batting. Trim the excess batting so that it butts up against the raw edges of the pressed prairie points.

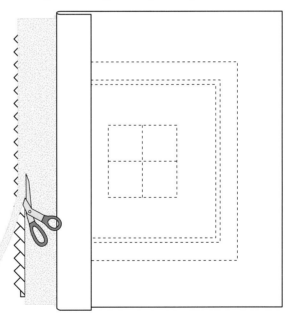

8. Trim the backing, leaving approximately ½" to ¾" to turn under.

9. Follow the directions on page 21 for making a sleeve. Center and pin the sleeve to the top edge of the backing only. Stitch the sleeve to the backing, using a ¼"-wide seam allowance.

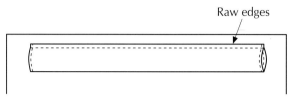

Raw edges

10. Fold the edges of the backing to meet the folded edges of the quilt top; pin. Check from the front to be sure none of the backing shows between the points. Blindstitch the backing, making sure the stitches do not go through to the front.

Fold

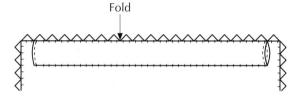

Hanging Your Bell Pulls and Wall Quilts

Hardware for bell pulls comes in two pieces. The piece at the top is the hanger; the one at the bottom has a small bell attached. Bell-pull hardware can range from very ornate brass to simple twisted wire pulls.

I hang my quilts most often with curtain rods because the rod does not show. Adjust the rod to a length slightly less than the width of the quilt. Using the small nails that come with the rod, fasten the rod to the wall.

Check out bed and bath stores for towel bars, and window-treatment departments for decorative rods with finials. Many wood craftspeople make decorative quilt racks and hanging clips.

Making a Label

Most quilters today understand the importance of documenting their work. I attach a label to the back of each quilt I make. The label should include your full name and as much information as you wish to add—the name of the design, the date (or at least the year), where it was made, whom it was made for, and any other interesting details. Your family or friends will appreciate this information, not only now, but in years to come; historians will need this information to identify your work.

To make your own label, use 100%-cotton fabric and a fine-line permanent pen. Follow the manufacturer's directions and test for permanency, bleeding, or fading by washing a test piece of fabric.

1. Prepare a piece of freezer paper by drawing guidelines, much like the lines on lined paper, with a dark marker.
2. Iron the freezer paper onto the back of the label fabric.
3. Write on the label, using the marked lines as a guide. It's helpful to place the fabric on a light box, but it's not necessary. Use a light touch and practice before writing on the actual label or quilt.
4. Hand appliqué the label, or use fusible web to fuse the label to the back of the quilt.

You might also enjoy embroidering your name and date directly on the surface of the quilt.

The Quilts

This chapter contains patterns and instructions for thirteen quilts and basic guidelines for two special memory quilts. You will also find directions for the bell pulls, with templates for five variations. All of the projects use either traditional or uneven Log Cabin blocks. Please read the front section of the book carefully before you begin any of the projects. You'll find the foundations for blocks that are foundation pieced on pages 91–96. Make enough copies of the foundations needed for your project. With some quilts, you have the option of strip piecing or foundation piecing the blocks.

The yardage requirements are based on 44"-wide fabric that has at least 42" of usable width. If your fabric has less than 42" of usable width, you may need more fabric. Cut all strips for the blocks, borders, and binding across the width, from selvage to selvage. For border-stripe fabrics, you will cut lengthwise strips.

The yardages specified are generous. Most call for 1/8 yard each of a number of different fabrics for the strips. You can, of course, use scraps or fat quarters. In fact, these quilts are ideal for using up scraps or leftovers from other projects. If you use scraps or fat quarters, be sure to cut enough strips to equal the total number of inches specified in the cutting instructions. For example, if the cutting instructions call for 6 strips, each 3/4" x 42", you will need strips that total at least 252" in length (6 x 42 = 252). Allow extra, since your strips will not be continuous. For a scrappy look, use as many different fabrics as possible in your blocks. The back sides of many fabrics can be used as solids for the center squares.

The yardage requirements for border-stripe fabrics may seem more generous than necessary, but border-stripe fabric is printed with the stripes running lengthwise. That means you will need a length of fabric equal to the length of the longest border in your quilt. The instructions do not tell you how wide to cut strips of border-stripe fabric because the cut width depends on the width of the stripe as it is printed on the fabric. When you cut the strips, be sure to include 1/2" for seam allowances beyond what you want to show on the finished border.

The finished dimensions for each quilt are "perfect measurements," meaning they are based on arithmetic, not the actual measurements of my quilt. In reality, your quilt will probably vary slightly from the perfect measurements.

The projects include appliqué templates for the flowers, leaves, stars, and other shapes used on some of the quilts. Appliqué templates do not include seam allowances because they are not necessary for the machine appliqué method I use.

You'll notice that some templates are the reverse image of the shapes as you see them in the quilt photos and quilt plans. That's because you trace the shapes on the paper side of the iron-on adhesive. When you fuse the pieces to the background fabric, they will be correctly oriented.

Be sure to review the directions for "Borders" on page 18 before cutting your border strips. It's especially important to measure the quilt through the center before you cut your border strips. This technique ensures a square quilt with straight borders. You will appliqué some borders before you add them to the quilt top. If you feel another motif is needed after adding the border, appliqué it over the seam.

25

Log Diamond with Floral Border

QUILT SIZE: 21" x 21"

FINISHED BLOCK SIZE: 1¾" x 1¾" ⚘ 16 TRADITIONAL LOG CABIN BLOCKS

The finished dimensions of your quilt will vary slightly, depending on the width of the border-stripe fabric you use for the fourth border.

You can make the Log Cabin blocks for this quilt using either the strip-piecing or foundation method. Follow the directions for the method you prefer. Before you cut your fabrics, use a highlighting pen to mark the directions for the method you have chosen. For the strip-piecing method, follow the directions labeled (SP). For the foundation method, follow the directions labeled (F).

Materials: 44"-wide fabric

⅛ yd. *each* or scraps of 10 to 12 lights and 10 to 12 darks for blocks

⅛ yd. or scraps of red solid for block centers

¼ yd. black solid for first, third, and fifth borders

¼ yd. light-background fabric for second border

½ yd. border-stripe fabric for fourth border

½ yd. red print for outer border and binding

Assorted scraps for appliqué

¾ yd. fabric for backing and sleeve

25" x 25" square of lightweight batting

Brown permanent pen for outlining and detail embellishment

Cutting

From the assorted light fabrics, cut a total of:
  12 strips, each ¾" x 21" (SP).
  12 strips, each ⅞" x 21" (F).
From the assorted dark fabrics, cut a total of:
  12 strips, each ¾" x 21" (SP).
  12 strips, each ⅞" x 21" (F).
From the red solid, cut:
  1 strip, ¾" x 21", for block centers (SP).
  1 strip, ⅞" x 21", for block centers (F).

The following cutting directions are for both methods:
From the black solid, cut:
  5 strips, each 1" x 42", for first, third, and fifth borders.
From the light-background fabric, cut:
  3 strips, each 2½" x 42", for second border.
From the border-stripe fabric, cut:
  4 strips, each 18" x the width of the stripe, plus ½" for seam allowances, for fourth border.
From the red print, cut:
  3 strips, each 3" x 42", for outer border.
  3 strips, each 2" x 42", for binding.
From the backing fabric, cut:
  1 square, 25" x 25", for backing.
  1 rectangle, 6" x 20", for sleeve.

Directions

1. Using the method of your choice, make 16 Log Cabin blocks. See "Strip Piecing" on pages 13–15 or "Foundation Piecing" on pages 10–13 for complete directions. For foundation piecing, use the foundation on page 92.
2. Using the quilt plan as a guide, arrange the blocks in a diamond pattern.
3. Sew the blocks together in horizontal rows. Press the seams in opposite directions from row to row.
4. Sew the rows together, making sure to match the seams between each block.

> *Tip:* Square up the quilt if necessary. If you have used the strip-piecing method, you may need to trim a little on some outer rows. Don't worry; it will not be noticed once you add the borders.

5. Add the first black border. See "Borders" on page 18.
6. It is easier to appliqué the flowers and leaves to the second border before attaching the strips. Measure the quilt lengthwise, including the first black border, through the center and cut 2 side borders to that length.
7. Prepare the appliqué pieces, using the patterns on page 28. See "Machine Appliqué" on pages 16–17 for complete directions. Using the quilt plan as a guide, arrange the flowers and leaves on the side border strips. Keep the pieces out of the seam allowances.
8. Fuse and appliqué the pieces to the border strips. Draw stems with the brown permanent pen to connect the flowers. Remove the stabilizer. Sew the appliquéd borders to the sides of the quilt top.
9. Measure the quilt crosswise through the center, including the appliquéd borders, and cut the top and bottom border strips to that length. Arrange, fuse, and appliqué the pieces as you did on the side borders. Draw the stems on the borders before removing the stabilizer. Sew the appliquéd borders to the top and bottom of the quilt top.
10. Add the third (black), fourth (border-stripe), fifth (black), and outer (red) borders.

11. Layer the quilt with batting and backing; pin-baste, using safety pins.

12. Straight-line quilt around the Log Cabin diamond, quilting diagonally between the light and dark sides of each block. Quilt in-the-ditch around the borders, ending with a row of quilting in the outer border, ½" from the fifth (black) border. Free-motion quilt around the leaves and flowers. See "Machine Quilting" on page 19.

13. Attach a sleeve, bind the edges, and label your quilt. See "Finishing" on pages 21–24.

Notes

Cut 12 tulips.

Cut 10 flowers and centers.

Cut 22 leaves.

QUILT SIZE: 21¼" x 23¾"

FINISHED BLOCK SIZE: 1⅞" x 1⅞"   🌹   22 FOUNDATION-PIECED LOG CABIN UNITS

Materials: 44"-wide fabric

⅛ yd. *each* or scraps of 6 to 8 lights and 6 to 8 red prints for Log Cabin units

⅛ yd. or scraps of red solid for block centers

¼ yd. black solid for inner border and Log Cabin units

¼ yd. gold print for Log Cabin units

Fat quarter of sky-blue background fabric

¼ yd. or fat quarter of grass or fence fabric

½ yd. dark red print for outer border and binding

Assorted scraps for appliqué

¾ yd. fabric for backing and sleeve

26" x 28" rectangle of lightweight batting

Brown permanent pen for drawing stems, tulip stamens, and outlining light flowers and hearts

Cutting

From the assorted light fabrics, cut a total of:
　　10 to 12 strips, each 1" x 21".
From the assorted red prints, cut a total of:
　　10 to 12 strips, each 1" x 21".
From the red solid, cut:
　　1 strip, 1" x 30".
From the black solid, cut:
　　2 strips, each ⅞" x 42", for inner border.
　　4 squares, each 4¼" x 4¼". Cut twice diagonally to make 16 quarter-square triangles for Unit A and Unit B; you will use 14.
　　10 squares, each 2½" x 2½". Cut once diagonally to make 20 half-square triangles for Unit B, Unit C, and Corner Unit.

From the gold print, cut:
　　4 squares, each 4¼" x 4¼". Cut twice diagonally to make 16 quarter-square triangles for Unit A and Unit C; you will use 14.
　　6 squares, each 2½" x 2½". Cut once diagonally to make 12 half-square triangles for Unit B, Unit C, and Corner Unit.
From the sky-blue fabric*, cut:
　　1 rectangle, 10¼" x 12¾", for background.
From the dark red print, cut:
　　3 strips, each 3" x 42", for outer border.
　　3 strips, each 2" x 42", for binding.
From the backing fabric, cut:
　　1 rectangle, 26" x 28", for backing.
　　1 rectangle, 6" x 20", for sleeve.
　　*Before you cut the background, fuse the grass or fence fabric to the sky-blue fabric. Cut a 1"-wide strip of fusible web and press to the wrong side of the grass or fence fabric. Cut a curved horizon line at the upper edge of the grass or fence fabric in the area covered by the fusible web. Fuse the grass or fence fabric to the background fabric.

Directions

1. Make the following Log Cabin units, using the foundations on page 93. See "Foundation Piecing" on pages 10–13 for complete directions.
　　　　10 of Unit A
　　　　4 of Unit B
　　　　4 of Unit C
　　　　4 Corner Units**
**Each corner unit has dark logs on 3 sides and light logs on the remaining side.
　　Leave the foundation paper attached until you have assembled the quilt.

2. Using the illustration below as a guide, join the Log Cabin border units to make the top, bottom, and side borders.

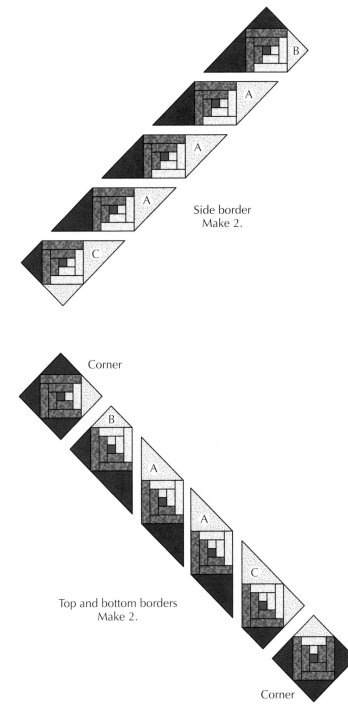

Side border
Make 2.

Corner

Top and bottom borders
Make 2.

Corner

Measure the Log Cabin borders. The side borders should measure 13½" long. The top and bottom borders should measure 16¼" long, including the corner units. Set the borders aside until you finish the center panel.

3. Add the inner black border to the background. See "Borders" on page 18.

4. Prepare the appliqué pieces, using the patterns on page 32. Using the quilt plan as a guide, arrange the pieces on the background. Fuse and appliqué the pieces. See "Machine Appliqué" on pages 16–17 for complete directions. Remove the stabilizer.

5. Add the side Log Cabin borders to the sides of the center panel. You can slightly ease or stretch the panel if needed. Press the seams toward the black border. Add the top and bottom Log Cabin borders.

6. Add the side outer borders, followed by the top and bottom outer borders.

7. Remove the foundation paper from the back of the blocks.

8. Layer the quilt with batting and backing; pin-baste, using safety pins.

9. Free-motion quilt the center section first, quilting around the tree trunk, leaves, flowers, and hearts. Quilt clouds or stipple quilt in the remaining background. Quilt in-the-ditch around the outer seam of the black border, the outer row of logs, and the outer seam of the Log Cabin border. End with a row of quilting in the outer border, ½" from the Log Cabin border. See "Machine Quilting" on page 19.

10. Attach a sleeve, bind the edges, and label your quilt. See "Finishing" on pages 21–24.

🦋 *Notes* 🦋

Cut assorted flowers, leaves,
and hearts to adorn the tree.

Sunshine and Shadows

by Donna Fite McConnell, 1995, Searcy, Arkansas, 68" x 75". Quilted by Phyllis Reddish, Anaheim Hills, California. While at the Museum of the American Quilter's Society in 1994, I saw an antique quilt in the Pilgrim-Roy collection that inspired me to create my own version of this popular design. It took 288 Log Cabin blocks, each 3½" x 3½".

Skinny Santa Bell Pull

by Donna Fite McConnell, 1995, Searcy, Arkansas,
8" x 25". I originally made this quilt for a Christmas
Santa challenge at the Arkansas Quilter's Guild.
The challenge rules allowed any kind of quilt,
as long as it contained a Santa.

Uncle Sam Bell Pull

by Donna Fite McConnell, 1995, Searcy, Arkansas,
8½" x 23". This bell pull was one in a series of
patriotic quilts I started designing in 1994.

34

Red Flower Bell Pull

by Donna Fite McConnell, 1997, Searcy, Arkansas, 6¼" x 20½". Because these bell pulls are small, they fit in with almost any decor.

Sunflower Bell Pull

by Donna Fite McConnell, 1997, Searcy, Arkansas, 7" x 20". After experimenting with different ways to make flowers, I designed this sunflower. It consists of two petal units, each a different shade of yellow.

Santa's Elf Bell Pulls

by Donna Fite McConnell, 1997, Searcy, Arkansas, 6" x 17".
The little quilt on the left is my first in a series of bell pulls that I began
making about three years ago. They make great gifts because they are fast
and easy to stitch. If you don't wish to draw a face, use preprinted
Santa fabric, as I did in the quilt on the right.

Angel

by Donna Fite McConnell, 1997, Searcy, Arkansas, 10″ x 21″. *Top and bottom
borders of uneven Log Cabin blocks give the illusion of a cathedral window. A sky-blue
fabric filled with clouds is a fitting backdrop for an appliquéd angel.*

White Star Flower

by Donna Fite McConnell, 1997,
Searcy, Arkansas, 15" x 17".
Shading with a permanent pen
helps make this little flower stand
out from the background.

Cherry Blossom

by Donna Fite McConnell,
1997, Searcy, Arkansas,
11¾" x 11¾". Four uneven
Log Cabin blocks, arranged
with the wider logs facing
inward, echo the circular
design of the appliqué.

38

Log Diamond with Floral Border

by Donna Fite McConnell, 1997, Searcy, Arkansas, 21" x 21".
Sixteen traditional Log Cabin blocks make up the center of this little quilt.
A floral border completes the design.

Families are like quilts,

Lives pieced together,

Stitched with hugs and tears,

Colored with memories and bound with love.

"Families Are Like Quilts …"
by Donna Fite McConnell, 1997, Searcy, Arkansas, 17¼" x 17½".
The message printed on this quilt was created using the photo transfer process (page 20).
Forty "two-row" Log Cabin blocks and an appliquéd border frame the verse.

Stems of Flowers

by Donna Fite McConnell, 1997, Searcy, Arkansas, 15½" x 20½". Sixteen traditional Log Cabin blocks border a design of machine-appliquéd flowers. A prairie-point edge finishes the quilt.

Tulip Garden

by Donna Fite McConnell, 1997, Searcy, Arkansas, 12¾" x 14½". I made these tulips from hand-dyed fabrics. A Log Cabin border, surrounded by a narrow border, accents the floral design. I embellished the background with a permanent pen.

Red Diamond with Stars

by Donna Fite McConnell, 1997, Searcy, Arkansas, 13½" x 17¾".
This patriotic quilt is the result of my experimentation with logs of different lengths.
A combination of short and long logs turns a traditional Log Cabin block into a rectangular one.

Patriotic Heart

by Donna Fite McConnell, 1995, Searcy, Arkansas, 21" x 21".
Thirty-six red, white, and blue blocks create a Log Cabin design that is both cozy and patriotic.

Miss India

by Donna Fite McConnell, 1997, Searcy, Arkansas, 11½" x 12½". Log Cabin strips border a photo transfer of my granddaughter in this simple little quilt. See page 20 for a description of the process.

Cali the Queen

by Donna Fite McConnell, 1997, Searcy, Arkansas, 11" x 11½". Log Cabin strips bring out the colors of my calico cat, Cali. She is one of three cats in our family. They think they need to supervise all that goes on in my studio.

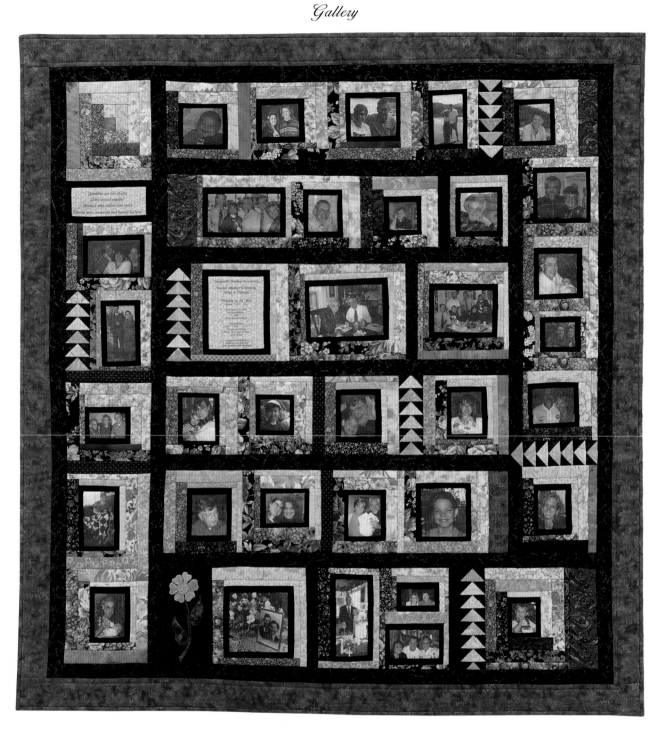

The Anniversary Photo Quilt

by Donna Fite McConnell, 1997, Searcy, Arkansas, 49" x 50". My parents celebrated their sixtieth wedding anniversary in October 1997. I made this quilt for them using thirty-four photo transfers. Log Cabin strips frame each photo. Flying geese and machine-appliquéd flower units add interest to the design.

"*Nobody Gets in to See the* WIZARD..."

by Donna Fite McConnell, 1997, Searcy, Arkansas, 23" x 25". When I first made this quilt, I planned to hang it in my workroom, but I gladly gave it away. My problem is that every time I make another, someone else wants it, and I still don't have one for myself. I used the photo transfer process (page 20) to add the verse.

Tree of Life – A Harvest of Love
by Donna Fite McConnell, 1997, Searcy, Arkansas, 21¼" x 23¾".
Twenty-four Log Cabin blocks, set on point, frame the appliquéd Tree of Life.

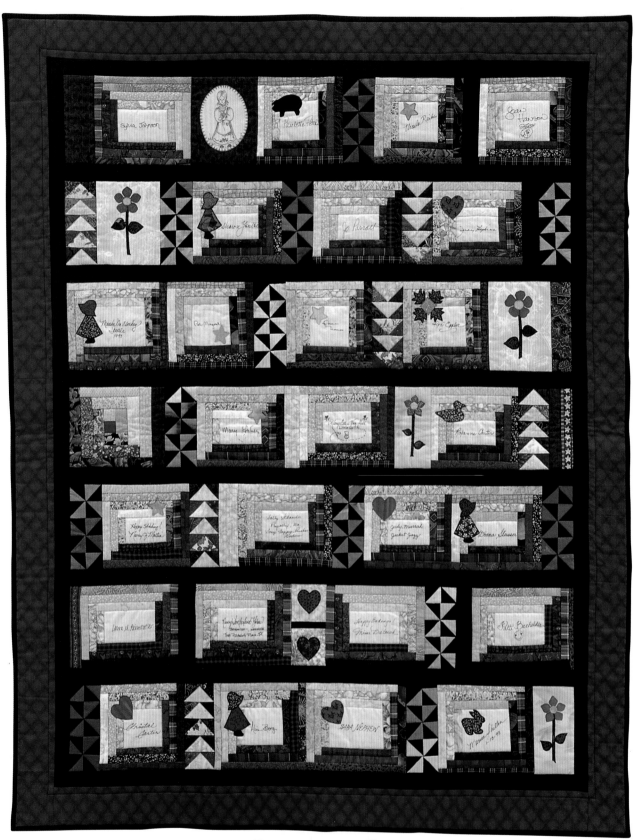

The Friendship Quilt

by Donna Fite McConnell, 1997, Searcy, Arkansas, 39" x 49".
I made this quilt from signature blocks I collected at an author's
workshop in 1993. Blocks left over from other projects complete the quilt.

Bell Pulls

A bell pull is a long, narrow, decorative piece of needlework that is usually hung by the door to replicate an antique bell pull. Before the invention of doorbells, bell pulls were used to let the resident of the house know when a visitor was at the door.

I started making these little bell pulls several years ago because my house has lots of windows and not much wall space. You can hang a little bell pull just about anywhere. They make wonderful gifts.

Skinny Santa Bell Pull

Size: 8" x 25"
Finished Block Size: 3⅝" x 3⅝"
2 foundation-pieced Log Cabin blocks

The finished dimensions of your project will vary slightly, depending on the width of the border-stripe fabric you use for the middle border.

Materials: 44"-wide fabric

⅛ yd. *each* or scraps of 5 light and 12 dark fabrics for blocks

¼ yd. black solid for inner border and appliqué

⅔ yd. border-stripe fabric for second border

¼ yd. Christmas print for outer border and binding

4¼" x 14½" piece of light print for Santa background

Assorted scraps for appliqué, including holly print*

⅜ yd. fabric for backing and sleeves

12" x 29" piece of lightweight batting

Brown permanent pen for drawing face

*If you are unable to find a holly print, use the templates on page 51. If you use a holly print, you may need to adjust the length of the background.

Cutting

From the assorted light fabrics, cut:
    8 strips, each 1" x 6".
    2 strips, each 1⅛" x 6".
From the assorted dark fabrics, cut:
    18 strips, each 1" x 6".
    6 strips, each 1⅛" x 6".
From the black solid, cut:
    2 strips, each ⅞" x 42", for inner border.
From the border-stripe fabric, cut:
    3 strips, each 22" x the width of the stripe, plus ½"
        for seam allowances, for second border.
From the Christmas print, cut:
    2 strips, each 1½" x 42", for outer border.
    2 strips, each 2" x 42", for binding.
From the backing fabric, cut:
    1 rectangle, 12" x 29", for backing.
    2 rectangles, each 4" x 7", for sleeves.

Directions

1. Make 2 Log Cabin blocks, using the foundation on page 92. See "Foundation Piecing" on pages 10–13 for complete directions.
2. Prepare the appliqué pieces, using the patterns on page 51. Arrange the pieces on the background fabric, using the quilt plan as a guide. Fuse and appliqué the pieces. Do not remove the stabilizer before you draw the face. See "Machine Appliqué" on pages 16–17 for complete directions.
3. Arrange the Log Cabin blocks with the light sides facing the Santa. Stitch the blocks to the Santa background.
4. Trim the sides to square up the piece if necessary.
5. Add the black inner border. See "Borders" on page 18. Add the second and outer borders.
6. Layer the bell pull with batting and backing; pin-baste, using safety pins.
7. Free-motion quilt around the Santa. Quilt in-the-ditch around the Log Cabin blocks and borders. End with a row of quilting in the outer border, ½" from the second border. See "Machine Quilting" on page 19.
8. Attach the sleeves, bind the edges, and label your bell pull. See "Finishing" on pages 21–24.

❧ *Notes* ❧

NOTE: The bell pulls pictured on pages 34–36 are similar to the Skinny Santa Bell Pull, with slight variations in the background and borders. You will need the same amounts of light and dark fabrics for the Log Cabin blocks, with the exception of the Sunflower Bell Pull; in this project, the light and dark logs are reversed. Use the foundation on page 92 and the appliqué patterns on pages 52–54 to make these bell pulls.

Skinny Santa

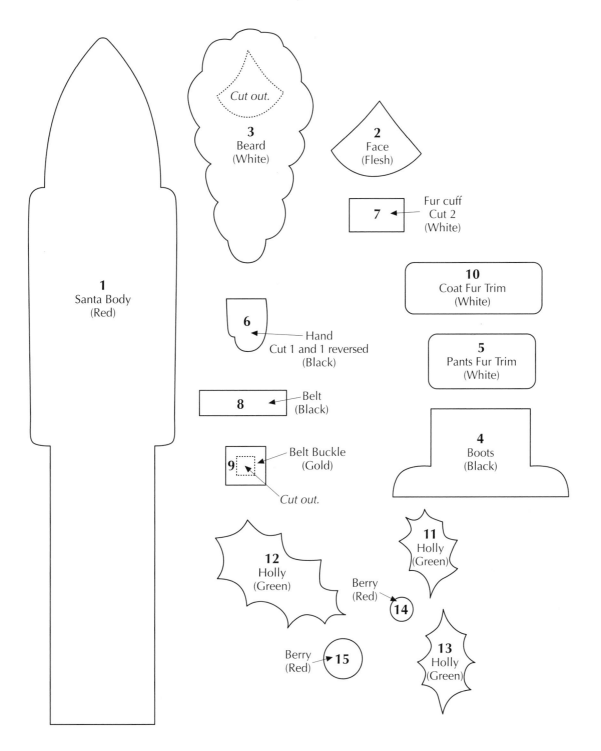

3
Beard
(White)

Cut out.

2
Face
(Flesh)

7 ← Fur cuff
Cut 2
(White)

10
Coat Fur Trim
(White)

1
Santa Body
(Red)

6 ← Hand
Cut 1 and 1 reversed
(Black)

5
Pants Fur Trim
(White)

8 ← Belt
(Black)

9 → Belt Buckle
(Gold)
Cut out.

4
Boots
(Black)

12
Holly
(Green)

11
Holly
(Green)

Berry
(Red) → **14**

Berry
(Red) → **15**

13
Holly
(Green)

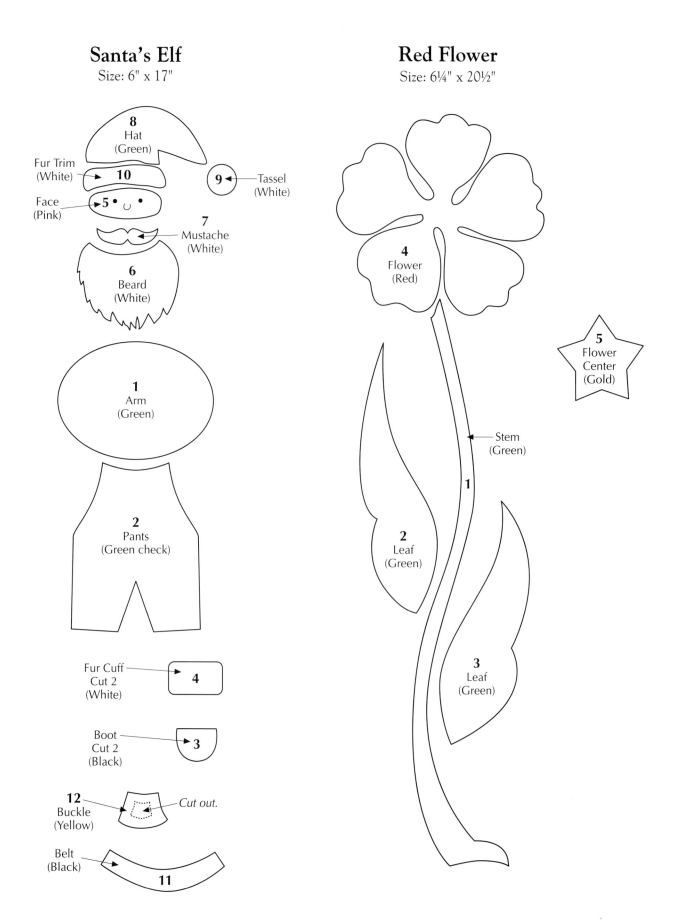

Santa's Elf
Size: 6" x 17"

8 Hat (Green)

Fur Trim (White)

10

9 Tassel (White)

Face (Pink) **5**

7 Mustache (White)

6 Beard (White)

1 Arm (Green)

2 Pants (Green check)

Fur Cuff Cut 2 (White) **4**

Boot Cut 2 (Black) **3**

12 Buckle (Yellow) *Cut out.*

Belt (Black) **11**

Red Flower
Size: 6¼" x 20½"

4 Flower (Red)

5 Flower Center (Gold)

Stem (Green)

1

2 Leaf (Green)

3 Leaf (Green)

Uncle Sam

Size: 8½" x 23"

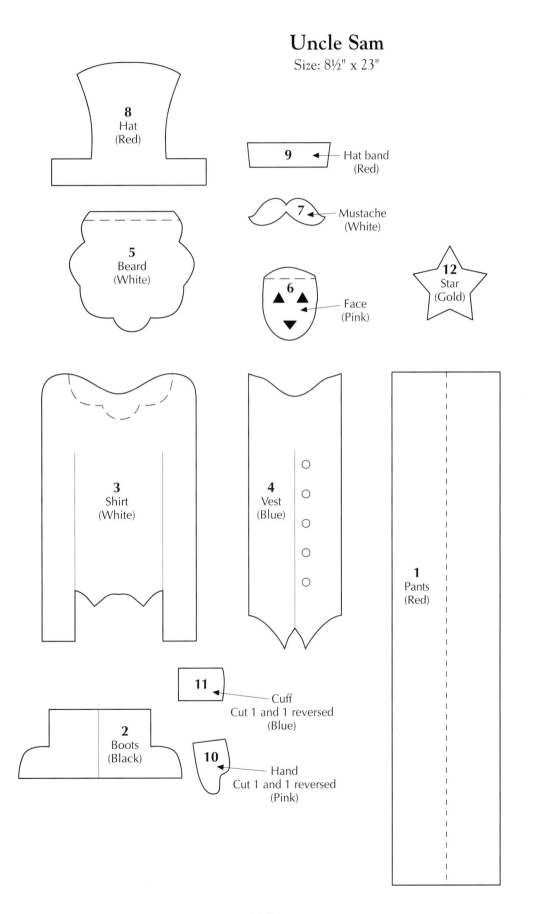

8
Hat
(Red)

9 ← Hat band
(Red)

7 ← Mustache
(White)

5
Beard
(White)

6 ← Face
(Pink)

12
Star
(Gold)

3
Shirt
(White)

4
Vest
(Blue)

1
Pants
(Red)

11 ← Cuff
Cut 1 and 1 reversed
(Blue)

2
Boots
(Black)

10 ← Hand
Cut 1 and 1 reversed
(Pink)

Sunflower
Size: 7" x 20"

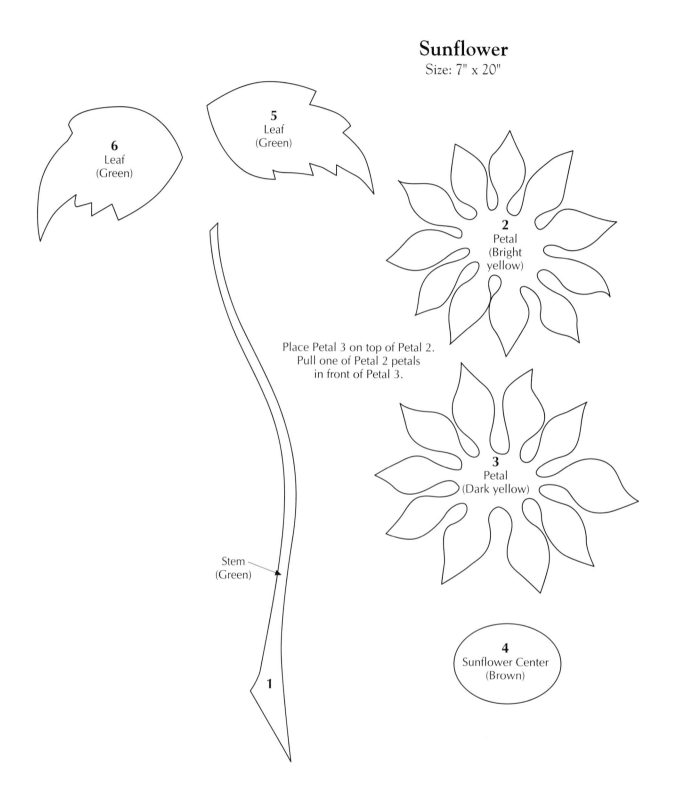

6
Leaf
(Green)

5
Leaf
(Green)

2
Petal
(Bright
yellow)

Place Petal 3 on top of Petal 2.
Pull one of Petal 2 petals
in front of Petal 3.

3
Petal
(Dark yellow)

Stem
(Green)

1

4
Sunflower Center
(Brown)

White Star Flower

QUILT SIZE: 15" x 17"

This quilt uses Log Cabin strips as a framing border.
Notice the placement of light and dark strips.

55

Materials: 44"-wide fabric

6" x 8" rectangle of light brown print for flower background

Assorted scraps for appliqué

Scraps of 6 light and 6 dark fabrics for Log Cabin border

⅛ yd. black solid for first and fifth borders

⅓ yd. floral print for outer border and binding

½ yd. for backing and sleeve

19" x 21" rectangle of lightweight batting

Brown, red, and yellow permanent pens for shading and detail embellishment

Cutting

All measurements include ¼"-wide seams.

From the assorted light and dark fabrics and black solid, cut:
    1"-wide strips, 8" to 13" long. Cut the strips to the necessary lengths as you add them to the flower background.

From the floral print, cut:
    2 strips, each 2½" x 42", for outer border.
    2 strips, each 2" x 42", for binding.

From the backing fabric, cut:
    1 rectangle, 19" x 21", for backing.
    1 rectangle, 6" x 14", for sleeve.

Directions

1. Prepare the appliqué pieces, using the patterns on page 57. Using the quilt plan as a guide, arrange the pieces on the background fabric. Fuse and appliqué the pieces. See "Machine Appliqué" on pages 16–17 for complete directions. Do not remove the stabilizer.

2. Use a brown permanent pen to shade one side of the leaves and stem with fine cross-hatching. Draw veins on the flower and leaves. Using the red and yellow pens, make dots in the petals next to the star center for stamens. Lightly outline the flower with the brown pen.

    Remove the stabilizer.

3. Add the black inner border. See "Borders" on page 18. Treat this unit as the "chimney" or center of a Log Cabin block.

4. Measure the length of the flower panel through the center, including the top and bottom black borders. Cut a 1"-wide light strip to this measurement and sew it to the right side of the unit. Measure again and add a light strip to the top of the unit, followed by a dark strip on the left side and a dark strip on the bottom. Continue adding light and dark strips until there are 3 complete rows of logs, ending with a dark strip on the bottom of the block.

5. Add another narrow black border.

6. Add the outer border.

7. Layer the quilt with batting and backing; pin-baste, using safety pins.

8. Free-motion quilt around the flower, leaves, and stem. Stipple quilt in the remaining background. Quilt in-the-ditch around each row of Log Cabin strips and each border. End with 2 rows of quilting in the outer border, stitching the first row ½" from the black border, and the second row ⅛" from the first row. See "Machine Quilting" on page 19.

9. Attach a sleeve, bind the edges, and label your quilt. See "Finishing" on pages 21–24.

❧ *Notes* ❧

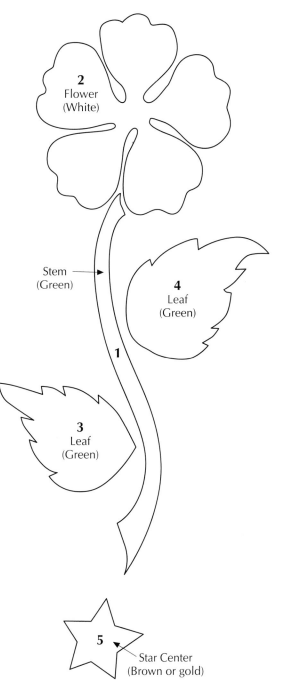

2
Flower
(White)

Stem
(Green)

4
Leaf
(Green)

1

3
Leaf
(Green)

5
Star Center
(Brown or gold)

Cherry Blossom

QUILT SIZE: 11¾" x 11¾" (NOT INCLUDING PRAIRIE POINTS)

FINISHED BLOCK SIZE: 3½" x 3½"

4 UNEVEN, FOUNDATION-PIECED LOG CABIN BLOCKS

Materials: 44"-wide fabric

⅛ yd. *each* or scraps of 8 to 10 assorted light pinks and 8 to 10 dark pinks for blocks and prairie points

Assorted scraps for appliqué

⅛ yd. black solid for inner border

⅛ yd. or fat quarter of pink floral print for outer border

Fat quarter for backing and sleeve

16" x 16" square of lightweight batting

Brown, red, and yellow permanent pens for drawing stamens and dots

Cutting

From the assorted light pinks, cut a total of:
    8 to 10 strips, each 1⅛" x 15".
From the assorted dark pinks, cut a total of:
    8 to 10 strips, each ⅞" x 15".
    1 strip, 1⅛" x 6".
From the black solid, cut:
    1 strip, ⅞" x 42", for inner border.
From the pink floral print, cut:
    1 strip, 2¼" x 42", for outer border.
From the assorted fabrics used in the quilt, cut:
    44 squares, each 1½" x 1½", for prairie points.
From the backing fabric, cut:
    1 square, 16" x 16", for backing.
    1 rectangle, 6" x 11", for sleeve.

Directions

1. Make 4 uneven Log Cabin blocks, using the foundation on page 95. See "Foundation Piecing" on pages 10–13 for complete directions. Leave the foundation paper attached until you assemble the quilt top.
2. Arrange the 4 blocks with the light logs facing inward. Sew the top 2 blocks together; press the seam to one side. Sew the bottom 2 blocks together; press the seam in the opposite direction. Join the rows.
3. Add the black inner border. See "Borders" on page 18.

4. Prepare the appliqué pieces, using the patterns on page 60. Using the quilt plan as a guide, arrange the pieces in the lower left corner of the blocks, starting with the branches and stems, followed by the leaves, petals, and flower center. Fuse and appliqué the pieces. Because you will be appliquéing with the foundation paper behind the blocks, you do not need a stabilizer. See "Machine Appliqué" on pages 16–17 for complete directions.

Tip: *Look closely at the photo on page 38 and you will see that I have used a satin stitch, varying the width of the stitch, making it thicker at the top of the petals. This variation gives the flower depth. Also note that the cherry blossom's center has a small crescent shape of darker yellow appliquéd to the lower edge to shade the center.*

5. Using the brown pen, lightly outline the cherry blossom and draw the stamens. Add shading to the branches and draw veins on the leaves. Make dots using the brown, yellow, and red pens.

Remove the foundation paper.

6. Add the outer border.

7. Layer the quilt with batting and backing; pin-baste, using safety pins.

8. Free-motion quilt around the stems, branches, leaves, and flower. Echo quilt a few rows around the design; then fill in the Log Cabin background with stipple quilting. Quilt in-the-ditch around each border, ending with a row of quilting in the outer border, ⅛" from the black border. See "Machine Quilting" on page 19.

9. Add the prairie points, attach the sleeve, and label your quilt. See "Finishing" on pages 21–24.

Notes

Stems of Flowers

QUILT SIZE: 15½" x 20½" (NOT INCLUDING PRAIRIE POINTS)

FINISHED BLOCK SIZE: 2⅝" x 2⅝"   16 FOUNDATION-PIECED LOG CABIN BLOCKS

Materials: 44"-wide fabric

5¾" x 11" rectangle of light blue fabric for background

Assorted scraps for appliqué

⅛ yd. *each* of 6 to 8 lights and 6 to 8 darks for blocks

⅛ yd. or scraps of dark pink solid for block centers

½ yd. border-stripe fabric for second border

¼ yd. dark print for outer border

Scraps of fabrics used in the quilt for prairie points

¾ yd. fabric for backing and sleeve

20" x 25" rectangle of lightweight batting

Brown, red, and yellow permanent pens for drawing stamens and dots

Cutting

From the assorted light fabrics, cut a total of:
    8 to 10 strips, each 1" x 42".
From the assorted dark fabrics, cut a total of:
    8 to 10 strips, each 1" x 42".
From the dark pink solid, cut:
    1 strip, 1" x 20".
From the border-stripe fabric, cut:
    4 strips, each 18" x the width of the stripe, plus
    ½" for seam allowances, for second border.
From the dark print, cut:
    2 strips, each 2½" x 42", for outer border.
From the assorted fabrics used in the quilt, cut:
    72 to 76 squares, each 1½" x 1½", for prairie
    points.
From the backing fabric, cut:
    1 rectangle, 20" x 25", for backing.
    1 rectangle, 6" x 14½", for sleeve.

Directions

1. Prepare the appliqué pieces, using the patterns on page 63. Using the quilt plan as a guide, arrange the pieces on the blue background. Fuse and appliqué the pieces. See "Machine Appliqué" on pages 16–17 for complete directions.

Tip: *I used a satin stitch on the flowers, varying the width of the stitch to make it thicker at the top of the petals. This variation gives the flower more depth. On two of the flowers, appliqué a small crescent shape of darker yellow to the bottom edge of the center for shading.*

2. Before removing the stabilizer, draw the flower stamens with a brown permanent pen. Make dots with the brown, yellow, and red permanent pens. Lightly outline the flowers.

3. Make 16 Log Cabin blocks, using the foundation on page 96. See "Foundation Piecing" on pages 10–13 for complete directions. Leave the foundation paper attached until you assemble the quilt.

4. Using the quilt plan as a guide, arrange the blocks to make the Log Cabin border. Join 4 blocks for each side border. Join 4 blocks for the top and bottom borders. Add the side borders to the appliquéd panel. Add the top and bottom borders.

5. Add the border-stripe border. See "Borders" on page 18.

6. Add the outer border.

NOTE: After I assembled my quilt, I used a decorative stitch (#23 on my Bernina 1260) and black thread to embellish the edge of the panel.

the-ditch between the seams of each border, ending with a row of quilting in the outer border, ½" from the striped border. See "Machine Quilting" on page 19.

10. Add prairie points, attach a sleeve, and label your quilt. See "Finishing" on pages 21–24.

7. Remove the foundation paper and stabilizer.
8. Layer the quilt with batting and backing; pin-baste, using safety pins.
9. Free-motion quilt around the stems, leaves, and flowers. Echo quilt a few rows around the design, then fill in the rest of the background with stipple quilting. Quilt a diagonal line between the light and dark sides of the Log Cabin blocks. Quilt in-

Notes

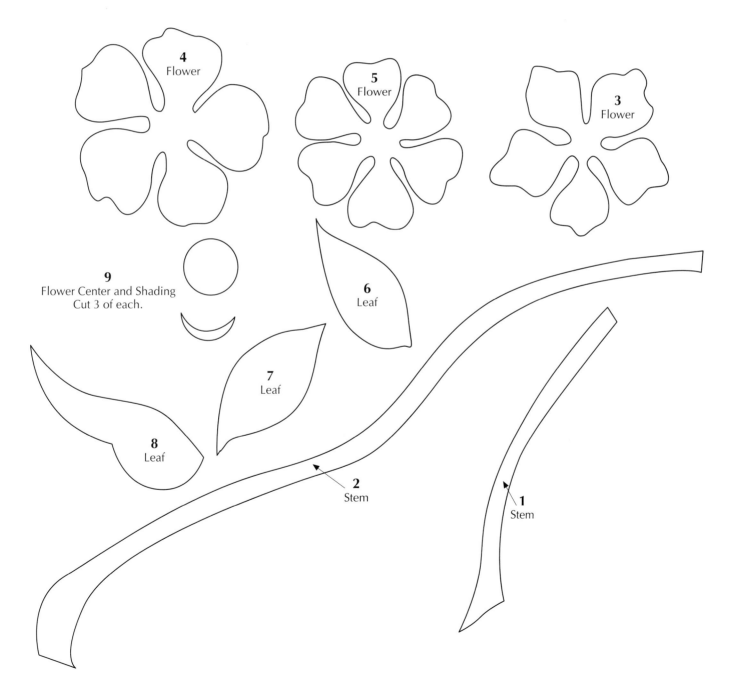

4
Flower

5
Flower

3
Flower

9
Flower Center and Shading
Cut 3 of each.

6
Leaf

7
Leaf

8
Leaf

2
Stem

1
Stem

Tulip Garden

QUILT SIZE: 12¾" x 14½"

FINISHED BLOCK SIZE: 1¼" x 1¼" ❧ 18 FOUNDATION-PIECED LOG CABIN UNITS

The finished dimensions of your quilt will vary slightly, depending on the width
of the border-stripe fabric you use for the two narrow borders.

Materials: 44"-wide fabric

⅛ yd. *each* or scraps of 6 to 8 lights and 6 to 8 darks for Log Cabin units

⅛ yd. or scraps of red solid for block centers

⅜ yd. border-stripe fabric for narrow borders

⅛ yd. light yellow print for Log Cabin units

⅓ yd. dark blue print for Log Cabin units, outer border, and binding

5¼" x 7" rectangle of sky fabric for background*

Assorted scraps of mottled, hand-dyed fabrics for appliqué

Fat quarter for backing and sleeve

16" x 18" rectangle of lightweight batting

Brown permanent pen for drawing veins in leaves, shading tulips, drawing grass, and outlining leaves

 *NOTE: The background panel, with the narrow border-stripe border added, must measure 5¾" x 7½" to accommodate the Log Cabin border. Therefore, the cut size of the background piece will be determined by the width of your border-stripe border. On my quilt, I cut the background piece 5¼" x 7" and the narrow borders ¾" wide; the entire background panel measures 5¾" x 7½", before adding the Log Cabin borders. If your border stripe is not the same width as mine, you will need to adjust the size of the background piece.

Cutting

From the assorted light fabrics, cut a total of:
    8 to 10 strips, each ⅞" x 21".
From the assorted dark fabrics, cut a total of:
    8 to 10 strips, each ⅞" x 21".
From the red solid fabric, cut:
    1 strip, ⅞" x 21".
From the border-stripe fabric, cut:
    8 strips, each 13½" x the width of the border stripe, plus ½" for seam allowances, for narrow borders.
From the light yellow print, cut:
    3 squares, each 3¼" x 3¼". Cut each square twice diagonally to make 12 quarter-square triangles for Unit A and Unit C; you will use 10.
    6 squares, each 2" x 2". Cut each square once diagonally to make 12 half-square triangles for Unit B, Unit C, and Corner Unit.
From the dark blue print, cut:
    3 squares, each 3¼" x 3¼". Cut each square twice diagonally to make 12 half-square triangles for Unit A and Unit B; you will use 10.
    10 squares, each 2" x 2". Cut each square once diagonally to make 20 half-square triangles for Unit B, Unit C, and Corner Unit.
    3 strips, each 2" x 42", for outer border and binding.
From the backing fabric, cut:
    1 rectangle, 16" x 18", for backing.
    1 rectangle, 6" x 11¾", for sleeve.

Directions

1. Make the following Log Cabin units, using the foundations on page 94. See "Foundation Piecing" on pages 10–13 for complete directions.
   - 6 of Unit A
   - 4 of Unit B
   - 4 of Unit C
   - 4 Corner Units**

   **Each corner unit has dark logs on 3 sides and light logs on the remaining side.

   Leave the foundation paper attached until you have assembled the quilt.

2. Using the illustration below as a guide, join the Log Cabin border units to make the top, bottom, and side borders.

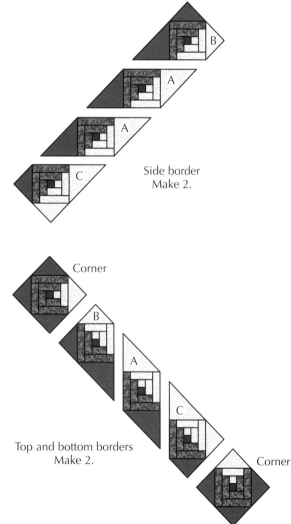

Side border
Make 2.

Corner

Top and bottom borders
Make 2.

Corner

Measure the Log Cabin borders. The side borders should measure 7½" long. The top and bottom borders should measure 9¼", including the corner units. Set the borders aside until you finish the center panel.

3. Determine the necessary dimensions for the background piece and the border-stripe border; see the "Note" on page 65. Add the border to the background piece. See "Borders" on page 18.

4. Prepare the appliqué pieces, using the patterns on page 67. Using the quilt plan as a guide, arrange the pieces on the background. Fuse and appliqué the pieces. See "Machine Appliqué" on pages 16–17 for complete directions.

   Before removing the stabilizer, draw veins in the leaves, shade the shadowed areas of the petals, and draw grass at the base of the flowers.

5. Add the Log Cabin borders to the sides of the center panel. You can slightly ease or stretch the panel if needed. Press the seams toward the narrow border. Add the top and bottom Log Cabin borders.

6. Add the second border-stripe border.

7. Add the outer border.

8. Remove the foundation paper from the back of the quilt.

9. Layer the quilt top with batting and backing; pin-baste, using safety pins.

10. Free-motion quilt the center section, quilting around the tulips and leaves. Outline or stipple quilt in the remaining background if desired. Quilt in-the-ditch around the border-stripe borders and the Log Cabin blocks. End with a row of quilting in the outer border, ½" from the border-stripe border. See "Machine Quilting" on page 19.

11. Attach a sleeve, bind the edges, and label your quilt. See "Finishing" on pages 21–24.

✤ *Notes* ✤

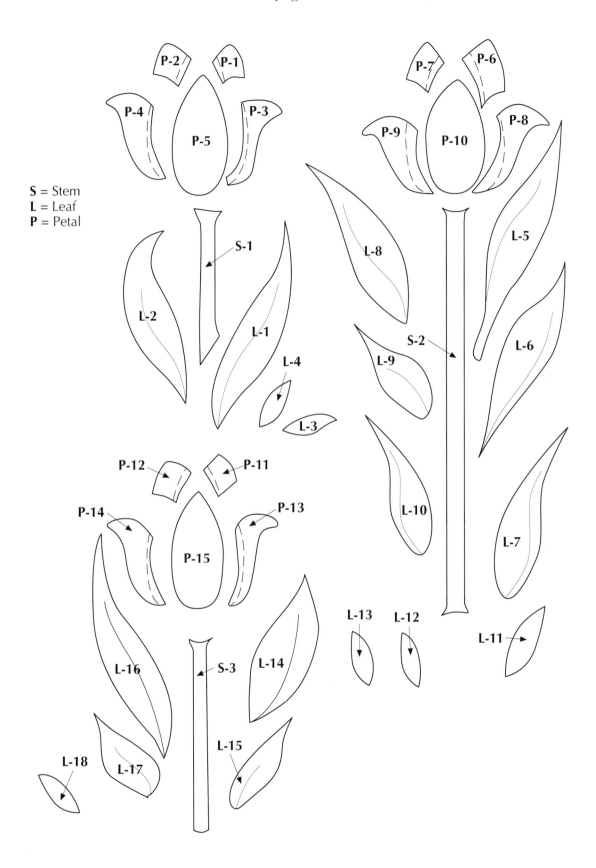

S = Stem
L = Leaf
P = Petal

Red Diamond with Stars

QUILT SIZE: 13½" X 17¾"

FINISHED BLOCK SIZE: 2⅝" X 4⅞" ❧ 4 RECTANGULAR, FOUNDATION-PIECED LOG CABIN BLOCKS

*The finished dimensions of your quilt will vary slightly, depending on the width
of the border-stripe fabric you use for the two narrow borders.*

Materials: 44"-wide fabric

⅛ yd. *each* or scraps of 10 to 12 white prints and 10 to 12 red prints for blocks

½ yd. border-stripe fabric for first and third borders

¼ yd. dark blue print or solid for second (star) border

Assorted scraps for star appliqué

⅜ yd. red print or solid for outer border and binding

½ yd. for backing and sleeve

18" x 22" rectangle of lightweight batting

Cutting

From the assorted white prints, cut a total of:
    10 to 12 strips, each 1" x 21".
    10 to 12 strips, each ⅞" x 21".
From the assorted red prints, cut a total of:
    10 to 12 strips, each 1" x 21".*
    10 to 12 strips, each ⅞" x 21".
From the border-stripe fabric, cut:
    6 strips, each 18" x the width of the stripe, plus ½" for seam allowances, for first and third borders.
From the dark blue print or solid, cut:
    2 strips, each 2½" x 42", for second (star) border.
From the red fabric, cut:
    2 strips, each 2" x 42", for outer border.
    2 strips, each 2" x 42", for binding.
From the backing fabric, cut:
    1 rectangle, 18" x 22", for backing.
    1 rectangle, 6" x 12½", for sleeve.
*Use a 1"-wide red print strip for the center rectangle (Piece #1) of each block.

Directions

1. Make 4 uneven Log Cabin blocks, using the foundations on page 91. See "Foundation Piecing" on pages 10–13 for complete directions.
2. Using the quilt plan as a guide, arrange the blocks into a diamond.
3. Sew 2 blocks together and press the seam to one side. Sew the remaining 2 blocks together and press the seam in the opposite direction. Join the rows, making sure to match the seams between the blocks. Leave the foundation paper attached until you have assembled the quilt.
4. Add the first narrow border. See "Borders" on page 18.
5. Cut the dark blue strips for the side border.
6. Prepare the appliqué pieces, using the patterns below. Using the quilt plan as a guide, arrange the pieces on the border strips. Avoid placing the stars in the seam allowances. Fuse and appliqué the pieces. See "Machine Appliqué" on pages 16–17 for complete directions. Remove the stabilizer.
7. Sew the appliquéd side borders to the quilt top.
8. Repeat for the top and bottom borders. If you like, appliqué a star over each seam where the borders meet.
9. Add the third and outer borders. Remove the foundation paper from the blocks.
10. Layer the quilt with batting and backing; pin-baste, using safety pins.
11. Quilt in-the-ditch between the Log Cabin blocks and around the perimeter of the blocks. Quilt in-the-ditch between each border. End with a row of quilting in the outer border, ⅛" from the third border. Free-motion quilt around the stars. Stipple quilt in the blue border background if desired. See "Machine Quilting" on page 19.
12. Attach a sleeve, bind the edges, and label your quilt. See "Finishing" on pages 21–24.

Cut 25 to 30.

🦋 *Notes* 🦋

Patriotic Heart

QUILT SIZE: 21" x 21"

FINISHED BLOCK SIZE: 1¾" x 1¾"   ❧   36 TRADITIONAL LOG CABIN BLOCKS

You can make the blocks for this quilt using either the strip-piecing or foundation method. Follow the directions for the method you prefer. Before you cut your fabrics, use a highlighting pen to mark the directions for the method you have chosen. For the strip-piecing method, follow the directions labeled (SP). For the foundation method, follow the directions labeled (F). To make a larger quilt, see the "Note" on page 96.

Materials: 44"-wide fabric

⅛ yd. *each* or scraps of 8 to 10 lights, 8 to 10 blues, and 8 to 10 reds for blocks

⅛ yd. of red, blue, white, or off-white solid for block centers

⅛ yd. black solid for first and third borders

⅛ yd. red print for second border

⅝ yd. patriotic print for outer border and binding

Assorted scraps for appliqué

¾ yd. fabric for backing and sleeve

25" x 25" square of lightweight batting

Cutting

From the assorted light fabrics, cut a total of:
    15 strips, each ¾" x 42" (SP).
    15 strips, each ⅞" x 42" (F).
From the assorted blue fabrics, cut a total of:
    10 strips, each ¾" x 21" (SP).
    10 strips, each ⅞" x 21" (F).
From the assorted red fabrics, cut a total of:
    10 strips, each ¾" x 42" (SP).
    10 strips, each ⅞" x 42" (F).
From the red, blue, white, or off-white solid, cut:
    1 strip, ¾" x 42" (SP).
    1 strip, ⅞" x 42" (F).

For both methods, cut the following pieces.
From the black solid, cut:
    4 strips, each ⅞" x 42", for first and third borders.
From the red print, cut:
    2 strips, each 1½" x 42", for second border.
From the patriotic print, cut:
    3 strips, each 3¾" x 42", for outer border.
    3 strips, each 2" x 42", for binding.
From the backing fabric, cut:
    1 square, 25" x 25", for backing.
    1 rectangle, 6" x 20", for sleeve.

Directions

1. Using the method of your choice, make the following Log Cabin blocks. See "Strip Piecing" on pages 13–15 or "Foundation Piecing" on pages 10–13 for complete directions. For foundation piecing, use the foundations on page 92.

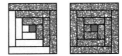

Blue/white   All blue
Make 4.   Make 3.

All white   Red/white   All red
Make 12.   Make 14.   Make 3.

2. Arrange the blocks in a heart pattern as shown in the quilt plan. Sew the blocks together in horizontal rows. Press the seams in opposite directions from row to row. Check the rows against the quilt plan to make sure that all blocks are oriented correctly.

3. Join the rows, making sure to match the seams between the blocks.

4. Add the first, second, third, and outer borders. See "Borders" on page 18.

5. Prepare the appliqué pieces, using the patterns below. Using the quilt plan as a guide, arrange the stars on the blue portion of the heart. Fuse and appliqué the pieces. See "Machine Appliqué" on pages 16–17 for complete directions.

6. Layer the quilt top with batting and backing; pin-baste, using safety pins.

7. Free-motion quilt around the appliquéd stars. Straight-line quilt around the edges of the Log Cabin heart and diagonally in the white areas. Quilt in-the-ditch of the borders. End with a row of quilting in the outer border, ½" from the third border. See "Machine Quilting" on page 19.

8. Attach a sleeve, bind the edges, and label your quilt. See "Finishing" on pages 21–24.

Cut 9 to 12.

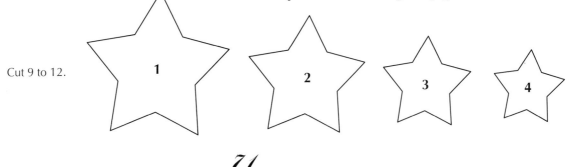

Angel

QUILT SIZE: 10" x 21"

FINISHED BLOCK SIZE: 2⅞" x 2⅞"

4 FOUNDATION-PIECED
LOG CABIN BLOCKS

The finished dimensions of your quilt will vary slightly, depending on the width of the border-stripe fabric you use for the inner border and divider strips.

Materials: 44"-wide fabric

⅛ yd. *each* or scraps of 8 to 10 lights and 8 to 10 darks for blocks

⅝ yd. border-stripe fabric or ⅛ yd. black solid for inner border and divider strips

7" x 12" rectangle of sky-blue or light fabric for background

Assorted scraps for appliqué

⅓ yd. Christmas or red print for outer border and binding

½ yd. fabric for backing

14" x 25" rectangle of lightweight batting

Brown permanent pen for face

Cutting

From the assorted light fabrics, cut a total of:
    8 to 10 strips, each 1" x 21".
From the assorted dark fabrics, cut a total of:
    8 to 10 strips, each ⅞" x 21".
    1 strip, ⅞" x 16", for blocks.
From the border-stripe fabric, cut:
    4 strips, each 22" x the width of the stripe, plus ½" for seam allowances, for inner border and divider strips.
If using black solid for inner borders, cut:
    2 strips, each ⅝" x 42", for inner border and divider strips.
From the Christmas or red print, cut:
    4 strips, each 2" x 42", for outer border and binding.
From the backing fabric, cut:
    1 rectangle, 14" x 25", for backing.
    1 rectangle, 6" x 9", for sleeve.

Directions

1. Make 4 uneven Log Cabin blocks, using the foundation on page 95. See "Foundation Piecing" on pages 10–13 for complete directions.
2. Using the quilt plan as a guide, arrange 2 blocks with the light logs facing inward. Join the blocks. Add a ⅞"-wide strip of dark fabric to each side of the unit. Repeat with the remaining 2 blocks. Leave the foundation paper attached until you have assembled the quilt.
3. Sew a strip of border-stripe fabric or a ⅝"-wide black strip to the top and bottom of each Log Cabin unit.
4. Prepare the appliqué pieces, using the patterns on page 74. Using the quilt plan as a guide, arrange the pieces on the background. Split the wings to widen their span slightly. Fuse and appliqué the pieces. See "Machine Appliqué" on pages 16–17 for complete directions.
5. Use a brown permanent pen to draw the face on the angel, making the face as simple as possible. Remove the stabilizer.
6. Join the appliquéd panel and Log Cabin units.
7. Add the side inner border strips to complete the inner border. See "Borders" on page 18.
8. Add the outer border.
9. Layer the quilt top with batting and backing; pin-baste, using safety pins.
10. Free-motion quilt around the angel. Stipple or outline quilt in the remaining background. Quilt in-the-ditch around the Log Cabin blocks and borders. End with a row of quilting in the outer border, ½" from the inner border. See "Machine Quilting" on page 19.
11. Attach a sleeve, bind the edges, and label your quilt. See "Finishing" on pages 21–24.

Notes

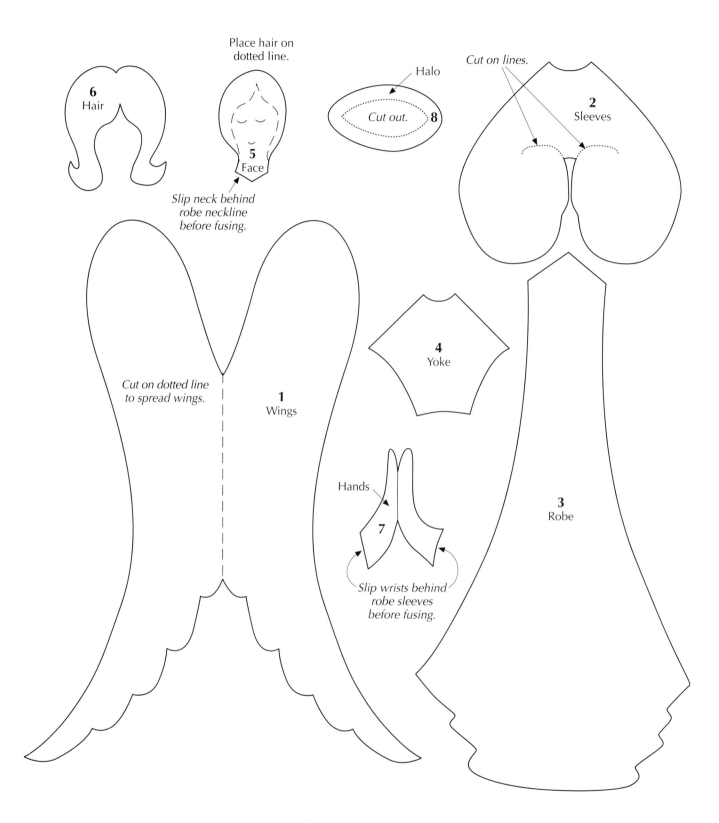

Place hair on dotted line.

6
Hair

5
Face

Slip neck behind robe neckline before fusing.

Halo

Cut out. **8**

Cut on lines.

2
Sleeves

Cut on dotted line to spread wings.

1
Wings

4
Yoke

Hands

7

Slip wrists behind robe sleeves before fusing.

3
Robe

Miss India

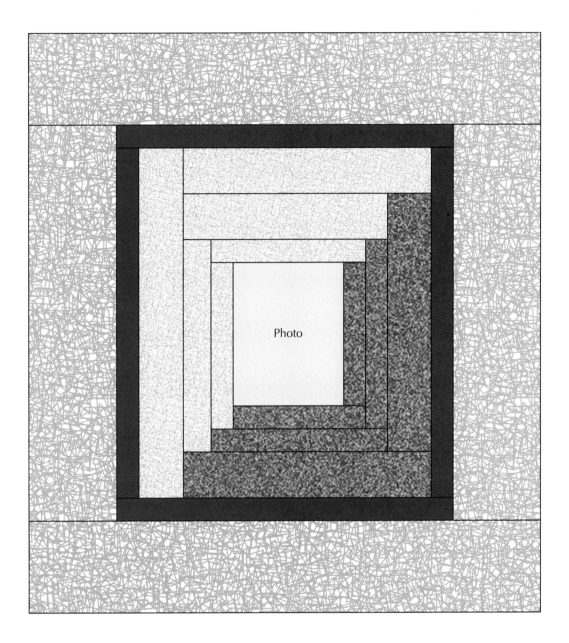

QUILT SIZE: 11½" x 12½"

The size of your quilt will vary,
depending on your photo.

This little quilt is very special to me. Miss India is my twelve-year-old granddaughter. We are very proud of her and are fortunate that she lives near us. India is an excellent student and very good on the computer. She is a great help to me and can get on her bicycle and be here in two minutes if I need her. She excels at both soccer and basketball.

I made a similar little quilt (page 44) featuring my cat Cali. You can use any favorite snapshot of a family member, a pet, or a special place for the photo transfer process (page 20). Print a caption for the photo on your printer or hand letter a caption on a piece of white paper and treat it like a photo. Follow the directions on page 76 to finish your little quilt.

 NOTE: You need access to a computer, printer, and color copier to make this project.

Materials: 44"-wide fabric

1 fat quarter of bleached or unbleached muslin. (Bleached muslin will give a slightly brighter image.)

3 strips of light prints, each 1" x 8"*, for Log Cabin border

4 strips of dark prints, each 1" x 8"*, for Log Cabin border

3 strips of light prints, each 1½" x 8"*, for Log Cabin border

2 strips of dark prints, each 1½" x 8"*, for Log Cabin border

1 strip of black solid, 1" x 42", for inner border

2 strips, each 2½" x 42", of print or solid for outer border

2 strips, each 2" x 42", for binding

1 square, 15" x 15", for backing (or size to accommodate your quilt)

1 rectangle, 6" x 10½", for sleeve (or size to accommodate your quilt)

1 square, 15" x 15", of lightweight batting (or size to match backing)

*You may need longer strips, depending on the size of your fabric photo. The center piece in "Miss India" measures approximately 2½" x 3¼" finished.

Directions

1. Transfer your photo to the muslin and your caption to a light strip, 1½" x 8". See "Color Photo Transfers" on page 20. If you plan to make more little quilts, copy as many photos and captions as you can fit on one sheet of photo transfer paper, being sure to reverse the images.
2. Cut out the photo piece, leaving a ¼" seam allowance on all sides.
3. Starting with a dark strip on the right edge, sew 2 dark and 2 light strips, each 1" wide, around the photo piece. For the next row of logs, also use 1"-wide strips, but end with the 1½"-wide light caption strip on the top edge. Finish the block with a row of 1½"-wide dark and light strips.

4. Add the inner black border. See "Borders" on page 18.
5. Add the outer border.
6. Layer the quilt top with batting and backing; pin-baste, using safety pins.
7. Quilt in-the-ditch around the photo and each row of logs, ending with 2 rows of quilting in the outer border. Place the first row ⅛" from the black border, and the second row ½" from the first. See "Machine Quilting" on page 19.
8. Attach a sleeve, bind the edges, and label your quilt. See "Finishing" on pages 21–24.

❧ *Notes* ❧

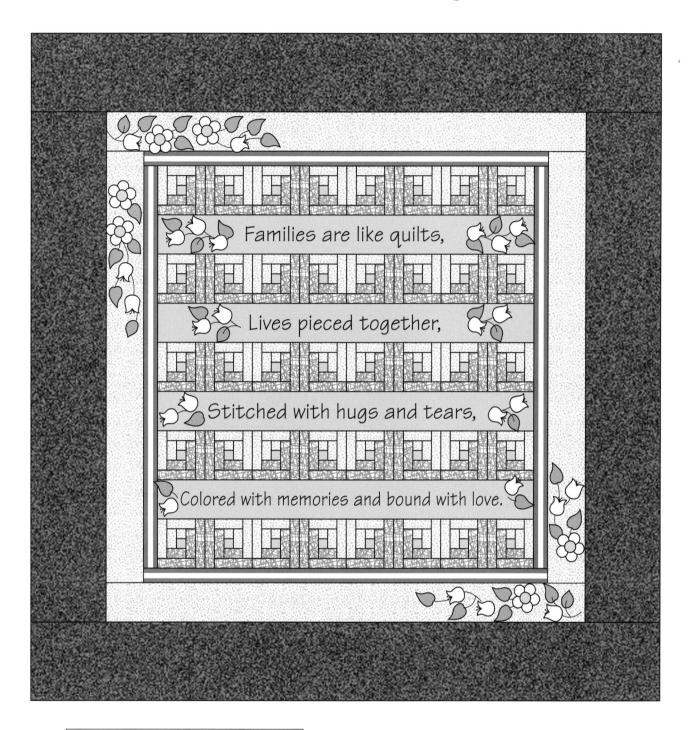

Families are like quilts,
Lives pieced together,
Stitched with hugs and tears,
Colored with memories and
bound with love.
Author Unknown

QUILT SIZE: 17¼" x 17½"
FINISHED BLOCK SIZE: 1¼" x 1¼"
40 FOUNDATION-PIECED LOG CABIN BLOCKS

Materials: 44"-wide fabric

⅛ yd. *each* or scraps of 6 to 8 lights and 6 to 8 blues for blocks

⅛ yd. or scraps of light blue solid for block centers

¼ yd. light blue mottled print for quotation strips*

⅜ yd. border-stripe fabric for inner border

⅛ yd. sky-blue fabric for second border

⅜ yd. dark blue print for outer border and binding

Assorted scraps for appliqué

⅝ yd. for backing and sleeve

22" x 22" rectangle of lightweight batting

Brown permanent pen for drawing stems, tendrils, and tiny tulip stamens, and outlining white flowers

*Use a print that won't interfere with the readability of the verse.

 NOTE: You need access to a computer, printer, and color copier, or permanent pen and freezer paper (for stabilizer) for hand lettering.

Cutting

From the assorted light fabrics, cut a total of:
    6 to 8 strips, each ⅞" x 42".
From the assorted blue fabrics, cut a total of:
    6 to 8 strips, each ⅞" x 42".
From the light blue solid, cut:
    1 strip, ⅞" x 42", for block centers.
From the light blue mottled print, cut:
    4 strips, each 1½" x 10½", for quotation strips.
From the border-stripe fabric, cut:
    4 strips, each 12" x the width of the stripe, plus ½" for seam allowances, for inner border.

From the sky-blue fabric, cut:
    2 strips, each 1½" x 42", for second border.
From the dark blue print, cut:
    2 strips, each 2½" x 42", for outer border.
    2 strips, each 2" x 42", for binding.
From the backing fabric, cut:
    1 rectangle, 22" x 22", for backing.
    1 rectangle, 6" x 16", for sleeve.

Directions

1. Make 40 blocks, using the foundations on page 92. See "Foundation Piecing" on pages 10–13 for complete directions. Leave the foundation paper attached until you have assembled the quilt.

2. Using the quilt plan as a guide, arrange the blocks into 5 rows of 8 blocks each in a horizontal Flying Geese pattern.

3. Sew the blocks together into rows; press the seam allowances open. (Pressing the seam allowances open puts the same amount of bulk on both sides of the seam, making it easier to join the blocks to the quotation strips.) The rows should measure 10½" long.

4. Print the quote, using a font of your choice, on your computer printer. Treat the printed quotation like a photo and use a color copier to transfer the words to photo transfer paper. See "Color Photo Transfers" on page 20. Remember to reverse the lettering so it will read correctly when transferred to the fabric.

 NOTE: You can also hand letter the words on the fabric strips, using a permanent pen. Before hand lettering, iron freezer paper to the back of the fabric to stabilize it.

5. Center each quotation transfer on a 1½" x 10½" light blue strip and transfer the words to the fabric.

6. Using the quilt plan as a guide, join the Log Cabin rows and quotation strips, alternating the rows and strips.

7. Prepare the appliqué pieces, using the patterns below. Using the quilt plan as a guide, arrange 16 tulips and 14 leaves on the quotation strips. Fuse and appliqué the pieces. See "Machine Appliqué" on pages 16–17 for complete directions.

8. Add the border-stripe inner border. See "Borders" on page 18.

9. Arrange the remaining appliqué pieces on the sky-blue border strips, keeping the pieces out of the seam allowances. Fuse and appliqué the pieces.

10. Before removing the stabilizer, outline the tulips and white flowers and draw the stems and tendrils with a brown permanent pen.

11. Add the appliquéd sky-blue border. Add the outer border.

12. Layer the quilt top with batting and backing; pin-baste, using safety pins.

13. Quilt in-the-ditch between the Log Cabin rows and the quotation strips. Straight-line quilt a diagonal line between the light and dark sides of each Log Cabin block. Quilt in-the-ditch around the borders, ending with a row of quilting in the outer border, ½" from the sky-blue border. Quilt ⅛" from the seams in the quotation strips and the sky-blue border. Free-motion quilt around the flowers and leaves. See "Machine Quilting" on page 19.

14. Attach a sleeve, bind the edges, and label your quilt. See "Finishing" on pages 21–24.

❦ *Notes* ❦

Cut 9 tulips for the border
and 16 for the quotation strips.

Cut 6 flowers
and flower centers.

Cut 21 leaves for the border
and 14 for the quotation strips.

"Nobody Gets in to See the WIZARD . . ."

QUILT SIZE: 23" x 25"

FINISHED BLOCK SIZE: 2⅞" x 2⅞" ❧ 12 UNEVEN, FOUNDATION-PIECED LOG CABIN BLOCKS

Materials: 44"-wide fabric

⅛ yd. *each* of 10 to 12 lights and 10 to 12 darks for blocks

Fat quarter of light-background fabric for center panel

Assorted scraps for appliqué

½ yd. border-stripe fabric for first border

⅛ yd. solid black for second border

⅝ yd. border-stripe fabric for third border

½ yd. print for outer border and binding

1 yd. fabric for backing and sleeve

27" x 29" rectangle of lightweight batting

Yellow buttons for flower centers, tiny black buttons for embellishment

NOTE: You need access to a computer, printer, and color copier, or permanent pen and freezer paper (for stabilizer) for hand lettering.

Cutting

From the assorted light fabrics, cut a total of:
    12 to 15 strips, each ⅞" x 21".
From the assorted dark fabrics, cut a total of:
    12 to 15 strips, each 1" x 21".
From the light-background fabric, cut:
    1 rectangle, 9¾" x 13½", for center panel.
From the border-stripe fabric for the first border, cut:
    4 strips, each 18" x the width of the stripe, plus
    ½" for seam allowances.

NOTE: You will cut the strips for the black border after you assemble the Log Cabin blocks and add the first border.

From the border-stripe fabric for the third border, cut:
    4 strips, each 22½" x the width of the stripe, plus
    ½" for seam allowances.
From the print, cut:
    3 strips, each 3" x 42", for outer border.
    3 strips, each 2" x 42", for binding.
From the backing fabric, cut:
    1 rectangle, 27" x 29", for backing.
    1 rectangle, 6" x 22", for sleeve.

Directions

1. Make 12 uneven Log Cabin blocks, using the foundation on page 95. See "Foundation Piecing" on pages 10–13 for complete directions. Leave the foundation paper attached until you have assembled the quilt.
2. Using the quilt plan as a guide, sew the blocks into 2 rows of 6 blocks each. Set these units aside until you finish the center panel.
3. Transfer the words on page 82 onto the center panel. See "Color Photo Transfers" on page 20.
4. Prepare the appliqué pieces, using the patterns on page 83. Arrange the flowers and leaves on the center panel. Fuse and appliqué the pieces. See "Machine Appliqué" on pages 16–17 for complete directions.

NOTE: Add buttons for the flower centers after you quilt around the flowers.

5. Add the first border-stripe border. See "Borders" on page 18.
6. The black second border requires a little calculation. Here's how to determine the cut width of the border strips:
    a. Start with the length of the Log Cabin border. Because you have made the blocks on foundation paper, the border strips should each measure 17¾" long.
    b. Subtract the width of the center panel (including the first border strips) from the length of the Log Cabin border.
    c. Divide that number by 2 to get the finished width of each border strip. Add ½" to that number to get the cut width of each strip. If, for example, your Log Cabin borders measure 17¾" long and your center panel, including the first border, measures 15" wide, you should cut your black border strips 1⅞" wide (17¾" – 15" = 2¾" ÷ 2 = 1⅜" + ½" = 1⅞").

From the black solid, cut 2 side borders and sew them to the center panel. Cut 2 top and bottom borders to the necessary lengths and sew them to the center panel.

7. Using the quilt plan as a guide, sew the Log Cabin borders to the top and bottom of the quilt top.
8. Add the third border.
9. Add the outer border.
10. Layer the quilt top with batting and backing; pin-baste, using safety pins.
11. Free-motion quilt around the letters in the quote and around the flowers and leaves. Quilt in-the-ditch around the borders, ending with a row of quilting in the outer border, ½" from the border-stripe border. See "Machine Quilting" on page 19.
12. Attach a sleeve, bind the edges, and label your quilt. See "Finishing" on pages 21–24.
13. Sew buttons to the flower centers. Add any other button embellishments as desired. On my quilt, I added tiny black buttons to balance the design.

Notes

L. Frank Baum

The Anniversary Photo Quilt

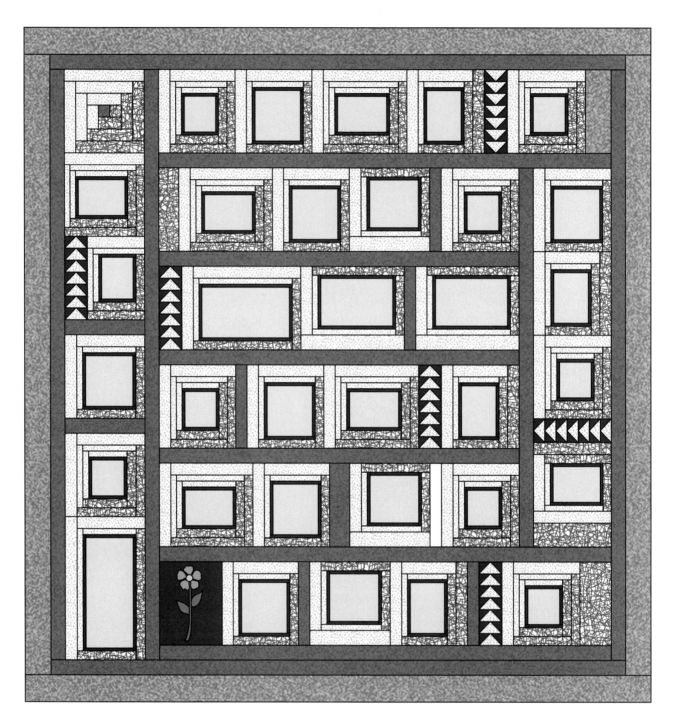

QUILT SIZE: 49" x 50"

While I was working on this book, my parents celebrated their sixtieth wedding anniversary. I made this quilt for them, using thirty-four family photos.

If you choose to make an anniversary (or other celebration) quilt, use fabrics to match the decor of the recipient. My mother's favorite colors are pinks and burgundies.

You'll need bleached muslin for the photo transfers, and light and dark fabrics for the Log Cabin blocks. For my quilt, I cut the following strips:

1"-wide light strips for Log Cabin blocks

1½"-wide dark strips for Log Cabin blocks

⅞"-wide black solid strips for framing fabric photos

1½"-wide various black print strips for vertical spacer strips between blocks

1¾"-wide black print strips for sashing and inner border

2¾"-wide strips for outer border

2"-wide strips for binding

1. Begin by transferring the photos and any words to fabric. See "Color Photo Transfers" on page 20.

2. Strip piece the blocks, using 2 light strips and 2 dark strips to complete each row of logs. See "Strip Piecing" on pages 13–15. To make the blocks consistent, sew the first strip to the same side of each fabric photo. (You may need extra rows or wider strips on some blocks to make them a uniform height.) Use 1½"-wide strips on the last round to allow for trimming if necessary.

3. Make Flying Geese units, using the foundation on page 96. See "Foundation Piecing" on pages 10–13.

4. Using any of the appliqué templates in this book, make flower units. See "Machine Appliqué" on pages 16–17. Make the units the same height as the blocks and whatever width you need to make the rows equal in length.

5. Assemble the rows of Log Cabin blocks, adding Flying Geese units, appliqué units, and 1½"-wide black print spacer strips as needed to make the rows equal in length. Scatter the spacer strips and units across the rows to balance the design. Join the rows, adding the 1¾"-wide sashing strips between the rows.

6. Add the inner and outer borders. See "Borders" on page 18.

7. Attach a sleeve, bind the edges, and label your quilt. See "Finishing" on pages 21–24.

Tip: *On a quilt this size, it is easier to quilt all vertical logs first, quilting in the same direction, then quilt all horizontal logs. It requires too much turning if you quilt each block continuously.*

The Friendship Quilt

QUILT SIZE: 39" x 49"

I made this quilt from signature blocks I collected when I attended an authors' conference at That Patchwork Place in 1993. I completed the quilt four years later and used it as an example in a workshop I taught on memory quilts.

I surrounded each signature block with light and dark strips. Flying Geese units (page 96), Pinwheel units, spacer strips, and pieced units left over from other projects served as fillers. I used assorted star, heart, flower, and animal appliqués to embellish the blocks.

You will need muslin or another light-background fabric for the signature blocks. As a general guide, I cut some squares 3" x 3" and some rectangles 2½" x 3½". For the Log Cabin blocks, you will need assorted light and dark fabrics. For my quilt, I cut the following strips:

1"-wide strips for Log Cabin blocks
1½"-wide black solid strips for vertical spacer strips, sashing, and inner border
3"-wide strips for outer border
2"-wide strips for binding

1. Collect signature squares and rectangles from friends or family for any special occasion. Prepare the blocks ahead of time by pressing the fabric to freezer paper. The freezer paper stabilizes the block, making it easy to sign. Ask participants to embellish their blocks with drawings if they wish.

2. Strip piece the blocks, using 2 light and 2 dark strips to complete each row of logs. See "Strip Piecing" on pages 13–15. To make the blocks consistent, sew the first strip to the same side of each signature square. On the smaller blocks, you will need to add logs or use wider strips to make the blocks equal in height. To make the rows equal in length, add the pieced units and spacer strips.

3. Make Pinwheel units as follows:
   a. From a black fabric, cut 5 squares, each 1⅞" x 1⅞". Cut once diagonally to make 10 half-square triangles. Cut 10 half-square triangles the same size from a fabric of your choice.

b. Join a black and a colored triangle to make a half-triangle square. Make 10 squares. Join the squares in pairs. Join the pairs to make 1 Pinwheel unit.

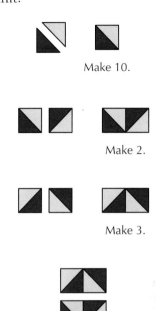

Make 10.

Make 2.

Make 3.

4. Make Flying Geese units, using the foundation on page 96. See "Foundation Piecing" on pages 10–13 for complete directions.

5. Using any of the appliqué templates in this book, make flower units. See "Machine Appliqué" on pages 16–17. Make the units the same height as the blocks and whatever width you need to make the rows equal in length.

6. Assemble the rows of Log Cabin blocks, adding Pinwheel and Flying Geese units, appliqué units, and 1½"-wide black spacer strips as needed to make the rows equal in length. Scatter the spacer strips and units across the rows to balance the design. Join the rows, adding the 1½"-wide sashing strips between the rows.

7. Add the inner and outer borders. See "Borders" on page 18.

8. Attach a sleeve, bind the edges, and label your quilt. See "Finishing" on pages 21–24.

Sunshine and Shadows

QUILT SIZE: 68" x 75"

FINISHED BLOCK SIZE: 3½" x 3½"   🌸   288 STRIP-PIECED LOG CABIN BLOCKS

This is the size of my quilt using the strip-piecing method. Your quilt may be different because slight variations in ¼" seam allowances multiply greatly in 288 blocks.

In August 1994, I saw an exhibit of Victorian quilts from 1875–1900 from the Paul D. Pilgrim and Gerald E. Roy collection at the Museum of the American Quilter's Society in Paducah.

One of the quilts in the show was an antique Log Cabin quilt made in 1875 by Rebecsa Gray of Lincoln, Illinois. Something about the glow of the quilt drew me from across the room. As I got closer, I saw that it was made of silks, satins, and velvets. I also realized that it was made from the same-size Log Cabin strips I have been using for years.

The description in the exhibit catalog reads:

"The work in this quilt exhibits not only this maker's ability to handle complex visual elements, but also her fine attention to workmanship. Her pre-occupation with small intricate piecing is evident in each example. In a traditional Log Cabin of this period one would expect the pieces to be 1" in width instead of the closer to ¼" width she has used here."

I stood in front of this quilt for several minutes, absorbing its beauty, and could not get it off my mind. On the way home, I said to my friends, "If Rebecsa Gray could make such a beautiful quilt in 1875 without rotary cutters and all of the conveniences we have today, I should be able to make a quilt this size."

When I got home, I drew the Sunshine and Shadows design on my computer, using a little sketch I had made. The result is the quilt you see here. My quilt has 288 Log Cabin blocks and is made of all-cotton fabric. Rebecsa's quilt had 292 blocks.

For more than two years, I carried the quilt top to show at lectures. When I started working on this book, I knew that I had to get it quilted. By then, I was having trouble with arthritis and could not hold the weight of the quilt. I entrusted my quilt to Phyllis Reddish, from California, an accomplished machine quilter. I am thrilled with the results.

For your quilt, I encourage you to use a wide variety of prints. The more fabrics you use, the more alive your quilt will look.

Materials: 44"-wide fabric

¼ yd. red or burgundy solid for block centers

3½ yds. total of assorted light fabrics, including prints with white background and yellow prints, for blocks

3½ yds. total of assorted dark fabrics for blocks

2 yds. total of assorted black prints for Logs #20 and #21

½ yd. red print for first border

2 yds. border-stripe fabric for second border*

6 yds. dark blue print or solid for outer border, backing, and binding**

Lightweight batting 2" larger than the quilt top on all edges

*Buy less and piece the borders if you prefer.

**By using the same fabric for the outer border, backing, sleeve, and binding, you can cut the borders and binding strips from the sides and bottom of the 6-yard piece. Use the extra fabric in the blocks.

The diagram below will work only if your quilt measures the same as mine or less. Buy more fabric, if needed, or use different fabrics for the borders and backing.

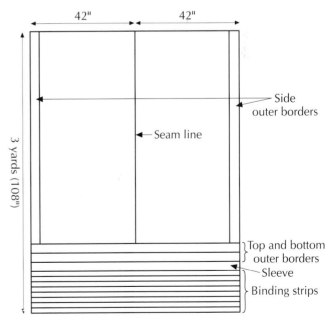

Cutting

All measurements include ¼"-wide seams.

From the red or burgundy solid, cut:
  8 strips, each 1" x 42", for block centers.
From the assorted light fabrics, cut:
  2 yds. into ¾"-wide strips for blocks.
  1½ yds. into 1"-wide strips for blocks.
From the assorted dark fabrics, cut:
  3½ yds. into ¾"-wide strips for blocks.
From the assorted black prints, cut:
  2 yds. into 1"-wide strips for blocks.
From the red print, cut:
  7 strips, each 2" x 42", for first border.
From the border-stripe fabric, cut:
  4 strips, each 72" x the width of the stripe, plus
  ½" for seam allowances, for second border.
From the dark blue print or solid, cut:
  2 strips, each 3½" x 75", along the lengthwise
  grain (see diagram on previous page), for side
  outer border.
  4 strips, each 3½" x 42", for top and bottom outer
  border.
  8 strips, each 2" x 42", for binding.

Directions

NOTE: I do not recommend the foundation-piecing method for this quilt.

1. Make 288 Log Cabin blocks. See "Strip Piecing" on pages 13–15 for complete directions. In the 120 blocks that make up the zigzag border, use assorted yellow prints for Logs #18 and #19. In the 168 blocks that make up the diamonds, use light prints with a white background for Logs #18 and #19. This variation creates definition between the zigzag border and the center section.

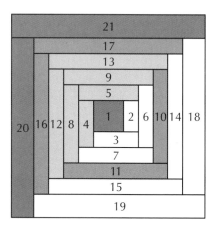

2. To make quilt assembly a little easier, arrange the blocks in one-fourth of the quilt at a time as shown below. Use the blocks with yellow Logs #18 and #19 in the outer 2 rows.

Upper edge

Left edge

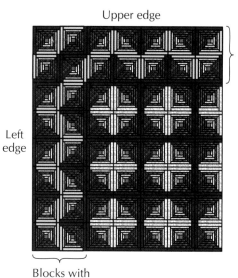

Blocks with yellow Logs #18 and #19

Blocks with yellow Logs #18 and #19

3. Sew the blocks together in horizontal rows. Press the seams in opposite directions from row to row.
4. Join the rows, making sure to match the seams between the blocks. Join the sections.
5. Add the first border. See "Borders" on page 18. Add the second and outer borders.
6. Layer the quilt top with batting and backing; pin-baste, using safety pins placed every 4" to 5" for machine quilting. Thread-baste in horizontal and vertical rows every 6" to 8" for hand quilting.
7. The easiest approach to quilting this quilt is to quilt diagonally through the centers of the blocks, dividing the light and dark sides. Quilt in-the-ditch around the borders, ending with a row of quilting in the outer border, ½" from the second border. Or, quilt as desired. See "Machine Quilting" on page 19.
8. Attach a sleeve, bind the edges, and label your quilt. See "Finishing" on pages 21–24.

Notes

Foundations

Red Diamond with Stars

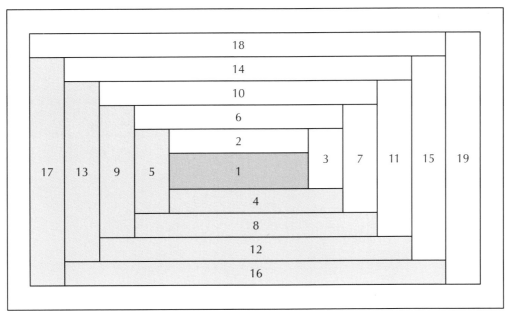

Foundation A
Make 2.

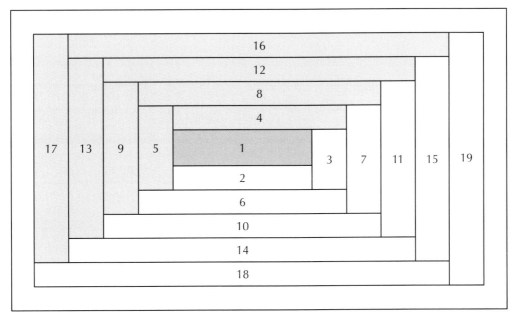

Foundation B
Make 2.

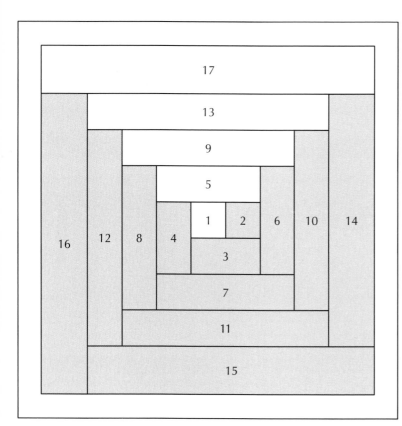

Note: For Sunflower Bell Pull (page 35), reverse the dark and light logs.

Bell Pulls

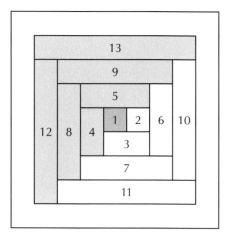
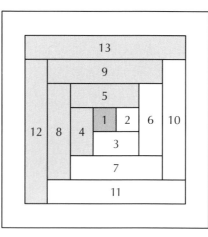
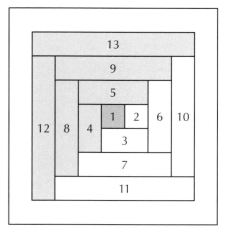

Log Diamond with Floral Border *and* Patriotic Heart

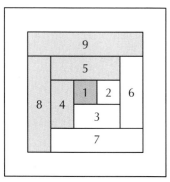
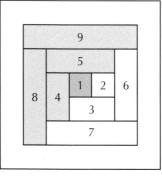
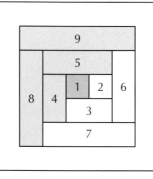
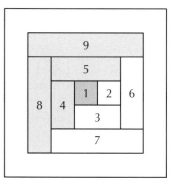

Families Are Like Quilts . . .

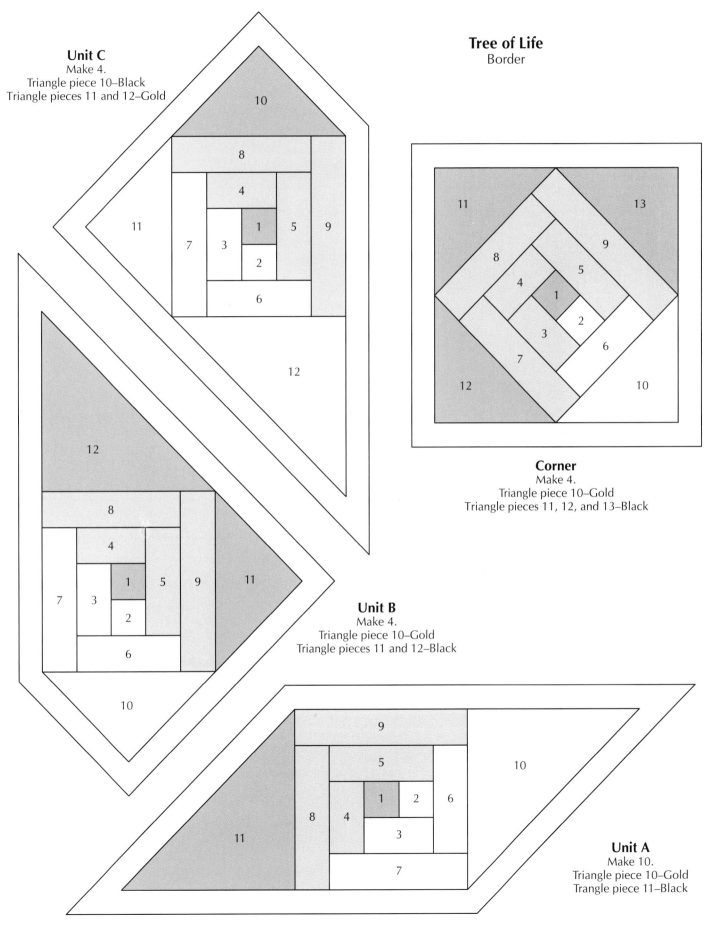

Unit C
Make 4.
Triangle piece 10–Black
Triangle pieces 11 and 12–Gold

Tree of Life
Border

Corner
Make 4.
Triangle piece 10–Gold
Triangle pieces 11, 12, and 13–Black

Unit B
Make 4.
Triangle piece 10–Gold
Triangle pieces 11 and 12–Black

Unit A
Make 10.
Triangle piece 10–Gold
Trangle piece 11–Black

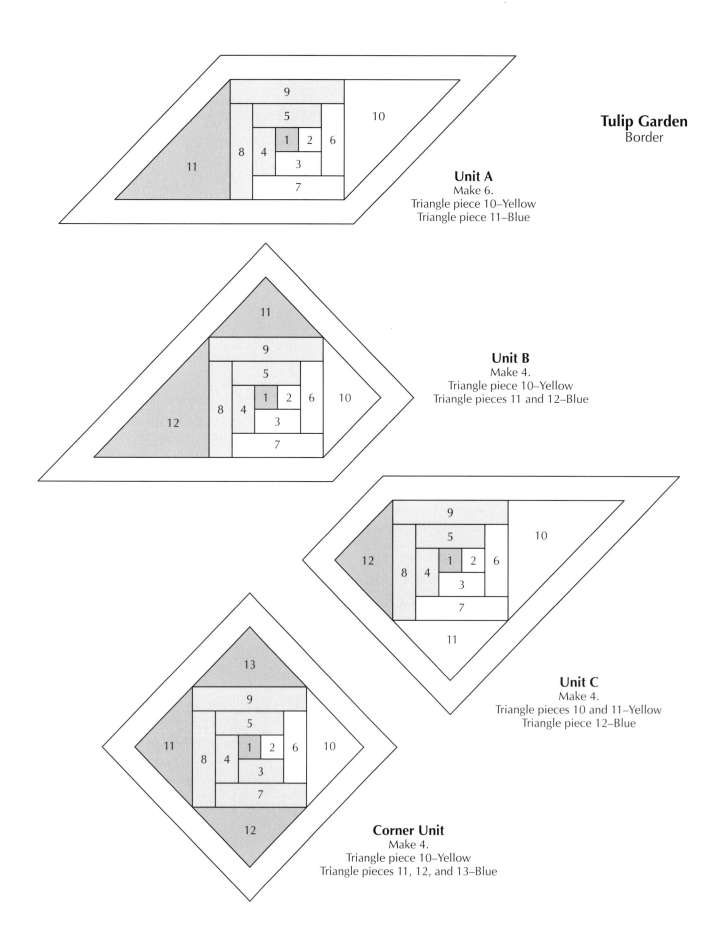

Tulip Garden
Border

Unit A
Make 6.
Triangle piece 10–Yellow
Triangle piece 11–Blue

Unit B
Make 4.
Triangle piece 10–Yellow
Triangle pieces 11 and 12–Blue

Unit C
Make 4.
Triangle pieces 10 and 11–Yellow
Triangle piece 12–Blue

Corner Unit
Make 4.
Triangle piece 10–Yellow
Triangle pieces 11, 12, and 13–Blue

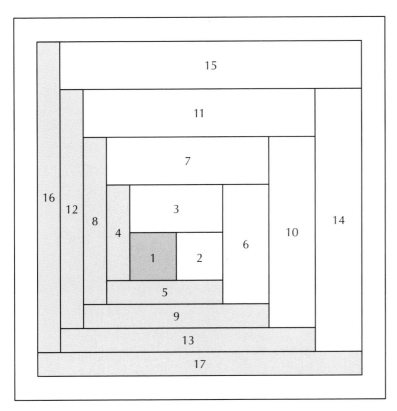

Cherry Blossom
Make 4.

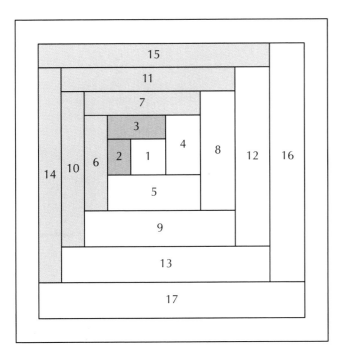

Angel
Make 4.

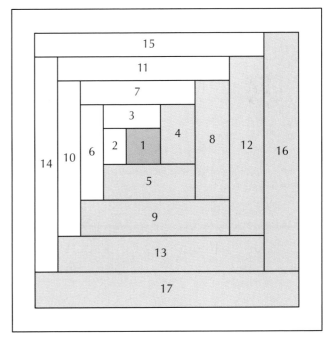

Wizard
Make 12.

95

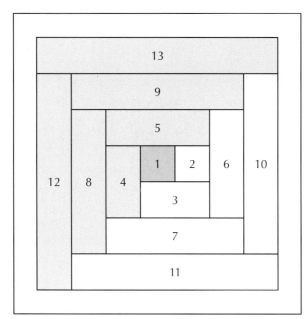

Stems of Flowers

Note: You can also use this foundation
for the Patriotic Heart (page 70)
if you want to make a larger quilt.
Follow the color placement diagrams on page 71.

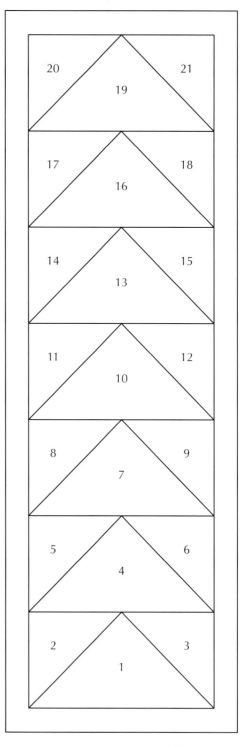

Anniversary *and*
Friendship Quilts
Flying Geese Unit

Note: Make as many as you need to balance the design.
In the Friendship Quilt (page 86), the units have 5 geese.
Add or subtract geese as needed.